MORE
WIRES AND WATTS

by Irwin Math

MORE WIRES AND WATTS

understanding and using electricity

irwin math

illustrations by hal keith

charles scribner's sons • new york

I would like to express my thanks to Hal Keith for his excellent execution of the drawings for this book. Additional thanks to Jerry Holtzman of the Bronx High School of Science for his comments and suggestions and to Clare Costello for her enthusiastic support.

Charles Scribner's Sons Books for Young Readers
Macmillan Publishing Company, 866 Third Avenue, New York, NY 10022
Collier Macmillan Canada, Inc.

Printed in the United States of America
First Edition   10 9 8 7 6 5 4 3

Library of Congress Cataloging-in-Publication Data
Math, Irwin.   More wires and watts : understanding and using electricity
  Irwin Math ; illustrations by Hal Keith.—1st ed.   p.   cm.   Includes index.
    Summary: Uses experiments and projects that produce actual working models to present the fundamentals of electricity and magnetism.
    ISBN 0-684-18914-3
    1. Electricity—Juvenile literature.   2. Electricity—Experiments—Juvenile literature.
  [1. Electricity—Experiments.   2. Experiments.] I. Keith, Hal, ill. II. Title.
  QC527.2.M36 1988   537—dc19   88–15767   CIP   AC

To Ellen, Robert, and Nicole, for the good times

CONTENTS

list of illustrations

foreword

During the first half of the twentieth century, American youngsters built club-houses, model cars, airplanes, and electrical and electronic devices of all kinds. Many were quite adept at figuring out how things worked without the benefit of specific instructions.

When one looks at the various playthings available to young people today, one is amazed by the incredible technical sophistication of the devices: electronic games, remote controlled boats and airplanes, dolls that walk and talk, and a host of mechanical devices. The addition of a few C or D cells promises all sorts of entertainment. But something is missing. The user is relegated to the role of button-pusher and observer. Even computers, the newest and most potentially creative devices, come with packaged, fully developed software that only needs to be run. There is not much to do in a creative sense and boredom quickly sets in. Even the "do-it-yourself" kit simply instructs the builder to put part A and part B into holes A and B, and so on. The principles of operation are omitted or at best passed off in a sentence or two.

Wires and Watts (Scribners, 1981) was an attempt to rekindle the creative spirit, to teach the fundamentals of electricity and magnetism through experiments and projects that produced actual working models. *More Wires and Watts* is written in the style of its predecessor, with the same philosophy of using common, easily obtained, inexpensive materials. The working models, all of which are new, are designed to function not only independently but as building blocks for more elaborate devices.

I.M.

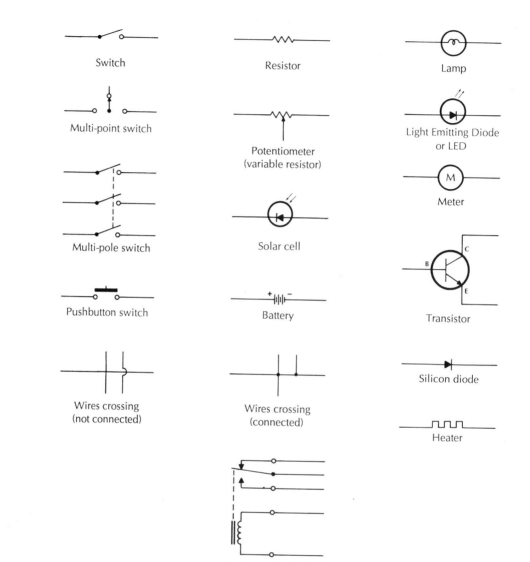

Switch

Resistor

Lamp

Multi-point switch

Potentiometer
(variable resistor)

Light Emitting Diode
or LED

Multi-pole switch

Solar cell

Meter

Pushbutton switch

Battery

Transistor

Wires crossing
(not connected)

Wires crossing
(connected)

Silicon diode

Heater

Electromechanical relay

Electrical symbols used in this book.

CHAPTER 1

WHAT IS ELECTRICITY?

The simple act of flicking a switch to turn on a lamp in a dark room is the result of thousands of years of scientific investigation and experimentation. The wondrous power of electricity that heats our homes, operates complex machinery, and produces convenience and entertainment for millions of people had its beginnings thousands of years ago in ancient Greece. There, a scientist by the name of Thales of Miletus, born in 640 B.C., observed an unusual property of amber, a plastic-type material commonly used for jewelry. When rubbed briskly with fur, pieces of amber (or "elektron" as it was called) would attract small bits of cork, wood, or similar objects in much the same way that a magnet attracts iron-based metallic objects. Not understanding why this occurred, Thales assumed that some unknown force was present in the amber. This force became known as electricity.

Duplicating these early observations is quite easy to do with a plastic object such as a comb to take the place of the amber, and a

FIGURE 1

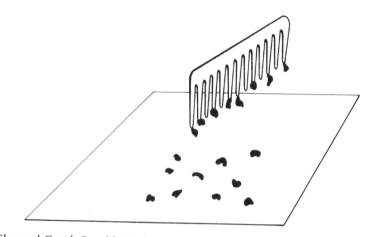

A Charged Comb Readily Picks Up Bits of Paper or Cork

warm, dry flannel cloth instead of the fur. This works best on a dry day. Holding the comb in one hand and the cloth in the other, briskly rub the comb a dozen times or so. Now bring the comb near some small bits of paper or cork and the pieces will "jump" to the comb (see Figure 1). This simple experiment, performed many years ago, started it all—but it was a slow start!

Until the eighteenth century, man's knowledge of electricity was limited to experiments not much more involved than the one we just performed. While many observations were actually made and theories proposed, nothing of a really practical nature resulted. By the end of the nineteenth century there developed a general opinion that electricity is the action of subatomic particles called electrons. Each electron has a negative ($-$) charge surrounding it. When these negatively charged particles are collected in abundance, as when the comb is rubbed with fur, static electricity is produced and the comb is said to be "charged with electrons." If the electrons are made to continuously move through a wire, current or moving electricity is produced. It is this second form (electric current) that operates our modern world and is the form that we will be concerned with.

It was not until 1791 that practical progress began. In that year an

Italian surgeon, Luigi Galvani, noticed that the legs of a frog he was experimenting with twitched every time he touched them with copper and zinc instruments. He noticed a similar result when exposing the frog to a strong static electric "charge," so he concluded that this action had something to do with "electricity trapped in the frog."

Although this conclusion was obviously wrong, Galvani's work made other scientists aware of this unusual occurrence. A few years later, in 1800, another Italian, Alessandro Volta, determined what had actually happened to Galvani's frog. Volta found that an entirely new form of electricity was produced whenever two dissimilar metals were brought in contact with each other in the presence of a strong, chemically active (often acid or base) liquid. The copper and zinc instruments of Galvani were the metals, and the body fluid of the frog was the chemically active liquid. The leg muscles were simply acting as the detector of this new discovery, which Volta called current electricity. Further experimentation led him to produce the first true source of continuous current electricity—the electric cell (incorrectly called a battery).

It is generally accepted that the work of Alessandro Volta was the single step that moved mankind into the modern world of electricity. The cell he created clearly demonstrated that electricity could be produced on a continuous basis. As a result, the electrical unit of potential or pressure, the "volt," was named in his honor.

To see how Volta's discovery actually worked, we require several easy-to-obtain items. First we need two dissimilar metals such as copper and steel. The copper can be common electrical wire and the steel can be a short length of coat hanger wire or even a knitting needle. Be sure to use solid wire and remove any insulation, covering, or paint so that both wires are bright and clean. This can easily be done with steel wool, sandpaper, or a file. For our "chemically active" liquid, a fresh lemon cut in half will do nicely. Finally, we will need a detector, and this we will have to build.

Figure 2 shows construction details of a simple detector that is inexpensive, easy to fabricate, and quite sensitive. All that is necessary

FIGURE 2

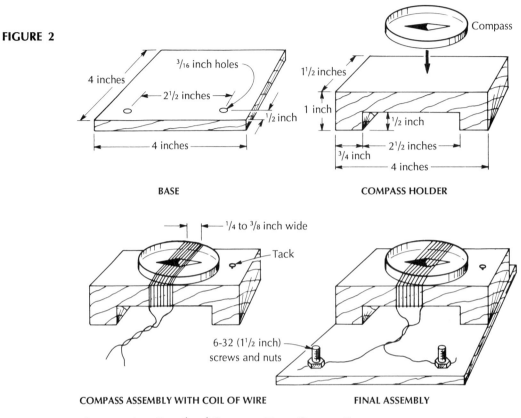

BASE

COMPASS HOLDER

COMPASS ASSEMBLY WITH COIL OF WIRE

FINAL ASSEMBLY

Construction Details of Compass-Type Current Detector

is a Boy Scout-style compass, 25 to 30 feet of thin insulated copper wire, a couple of 6-32 by 1½-inch long machine screws and nuts, and two small pieces of wood. The wire should be between #24 and #30 gauge and can be obtained from an electrical supply house or an old radio or TV loudspeaker transformer. The wire must be insulated, except for ½-inch at each end. Use sandpaper, a file, or a knife to scrape away the insulation.

To begin construction, cut the two pieces of wood as shown in the figure. Then glue the compass to the U-shaped piece of wood, wind the wire around the wood and compass carefully, and secure it in place by twisting the leads as shown. Now glue the compass assembly to the base and connect the two leads to the machine screw "ter-

FIGURE 3

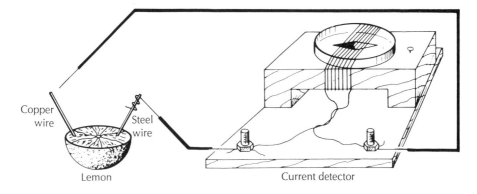

An Ultra-Simple Lemon Battery

minals.'' Finally, coat the wire turns with a thin layer of shellac or varnish to hold them permanently in place, and the detector is finished. As an option, a small carpet tack can be pressed into the assembly as shown to keep the compass needle oriented properly with no current flow.

Now let's duplicate Volta's discovery. Referring to Figure 3, push the steel and copper wires a short distance into the lemon. Connect a short piece of wire from the compass detector to the steel wire. Connect another short piece of wire to the other terminal of the compass detector and hold this in your hand. Hold the compass so that the needle is parallel to the turns of wire and allow it to come to rest. Now touch the free wire to the copper wire in the lemon and see what happens to the compass. The violent movement indicates the production of current electricity. If you have a pair of earphones, connecting them to the lemon-cell will produce loud clicks as well.

Volta's original cell worked on this exact principle. The only difference was that he used copper and zinc disks and, sandwiched between the disks, paper that had been soaked in salt-water.

The effect of Volta's discovery on the scientific world was immediate. At last scientists had a continuous source of electricity to work with, and progress was rapid. In 1819, a Danish scientist, Hans Christian Oersted, discovered that there was a direct relationship between

FIGURE 4

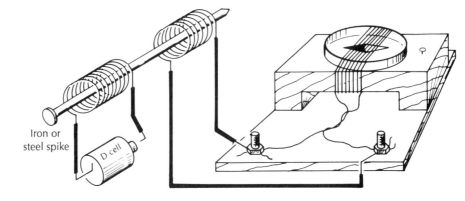

Iron or
steel spike

Demonstration of Michael Faraday's Famous Experiment

electricity and magnetism by observing that a compass needle would move when brought near a wire in which an electric current was flowing—just like our compass detector. Shortly thereafter, Michael Faraday proved that electricity could be converted into magnetism and vice-versa by a famous and important experiment that we can easily repeat. Figure 4 shows the experiment.

On a ¼-inch by 6-inch steel or iron nail, easily obtained from most lumber yards or building supply shops, wind two coils of about 20 turns each of common bell wire, leaving a 2-inch space between the coils. Connect one of the coils to the compass detector and the other one to a common D cell as shown.

If you now alternately interrupt the electric circuit by rapidly touching one of the wires to the cell terminal and then removing it, you will notice that the compass needle jumps back and forth. The current flowing in the coil connected to the cell causes the nail to become magnetized. The magnetic field then travels through the nail and acts on the second coil, where it is converted back into an electrical current. This experiment demonstrates the principles that led other scientists to the development of the transformer, generator, and electric motor a short time thereafter.

During the last half of the 1800s many of the laws regarding current electricity were formulated, and by the early 1900s the age of electricity had been established.

CHAPTER 2

LET'S GET DOWN TO basics

Although no one has ever seen electricity, learning to use it properly need not be difficult. Understanding a few basic principles can make the difference between the successful experimenter and the disappointed amateur. Let us begin with a few facts that will be useful in our future experimenting.

Always remember that if a metal path is present, electricity flows—just like a liquid. In fact, the flow of electricity through a wire can be compared to the flow of water through a pipe. If you drilled a

FIGURE 5

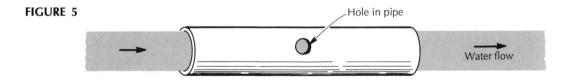

Water Pipe Analogy

hole in the side of a pipe (Figure 5) and looked in, you would see a certain amount of water passing your viewing point each second, producing a water current like the current in a river. Stick your finger in the hole in the pipe and you would feel the push, or "strength," of the current. This strength is determined by how much force or pressure or potential is being applied at the end of the pipe.

A wire with electrons flowing through it has similar characteristics. The flow of electrons is called electric current. The strength of this current is also determined by the amount of pressure applied to the wire—in this case, electric potential or pressure.

In the water system, the current is measured in gallons moving through a cross section of pipe per second. Water pressure is measured in pounds per square inch. Electrical current is measured in the number of electrons flowing through a cross section of wire in units called amperes. Pressure is measured in units called volts. In either system, the higher the pressure, the greater the current.

Unlike the water example, it is not enough for an electric current to flow by just applying pressure (voltage). The current must flow in a complete path, or circuit, from its source, through the wires and other components, and back to the source. Any break or interruption in the circuit will stop the flow.

Figure 6 shows a simple electric circuit where the current flows from the cell negative (−) terminal, through the switch (when it is closed), through the light bulb, and finally back to the cell positive (+) terminal. This is the circuit of the common flashlight. If you break the circuit by opening the switch, or if there is a break in the wires, the flow of current will stop and the bulb will go out. When a light bulb "burns out," it is usually because the thin filament in the bulb has been broken and the path through the bulb is interrupted.

Whether the circuit is a simple flashlight or the complicated hookup from an electrical power generating station to your home, the circuit must be complete. This is why the power cord connected to all home appliances has at least two wires, one for incoming electron flow, the other for outgoing flow.

FIGURE 6

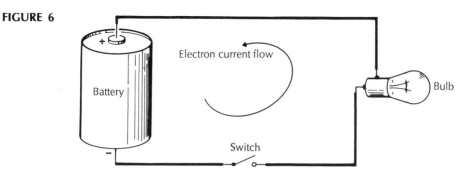

Flashlight Circuit

A simple experiment will demonstrate this. A few common items, which are easy to obtain, are needed: a 1.5-volt dry cell, a length of common bell wire, a 1.5-volt, #222 flashlight bulb with matching socket. All of these are available from your local electrical supply store such as Radio Shack or the electrical section of a department store such as Sears. Carefully remove some covering from each end of two 12-inch lengths of wire and hook up the circuit shown in Figure 7. Connect one wire to the cell, but leave the other end of this wire unconnected, as shown in the diagram. The bulb will not light be-

FIGURE 7

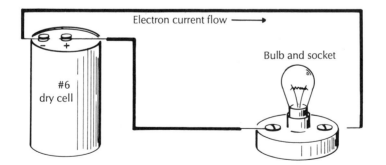

Complete-Circuit Experiment

cause there is no complete path. Now connect the open wire to the remaining screw on the socket, and the bulb will light.

Electric current will only flow through certain materials called conductors. Almost all metals, and particularly copper (the metal most wires are made of), are good conductors. A material that electricity cannot flow through is called an insulator. The covering on the wire used to hook up the light bulb circuit is an insulator. It is used to keep the current inside the wire and prevent it from flowing to adjacent wires if the wires accidentally touch.

The light bulb circuit can easily be modified to help us explore which materials are insulators and which are conductors. Cut another 12-inch length of wire and reconnect the circuit as shown in Figure 8. The bulb will not light with the two wires unconnected. If a conductor of electricity is placed between the two wires, the circuit will be completed and the bulb will light. Using this simple conductivity tester, we can experiment with glass, plastic, wood, rubber, and various metals to determine which are conductors and which are insulators.

Not all conductors are metals. Liquids such as water may also conduct electricity, depending on what has been dissolved in the water. Pure water will not conduct. To see this, place the two wires from the tester into a glass half-filled with pure water. Now add one to two tablespoons of table salt to the water. The dissolved salt increases conduction to the point where the bulb will light.

FIGURE 8

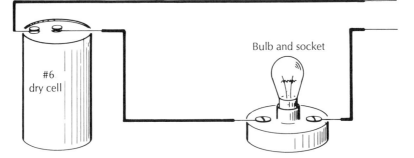

Insulator/Conductor Tester

FIGURE 9

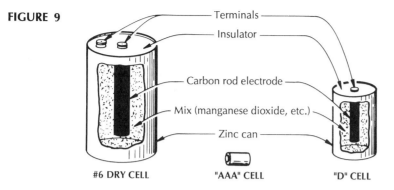

#6 DRY CELL   "AAA" CELL   "D" CELL

Cutaway View of Two Common Dry Cells

Now empty the glass and rinse it thoroughly. Repeat the above procedure, but this time use granulated table sugar. The bulb does not light because the sugar-water solution is not a conductor.

The cell in our experiment has an electrical pressure of only 1.5 volts. If the voltage were much higher (for example, the 115 volts from a common household outlet), plain tap water would not only light a bulb but could shock and even seriously injure a person standing in a puddle of water if that person happened to touch a faulty electrical appliance. That is because most tap water has some small amounts of salts and minerals in solution.

Electricity can be produced in many ways. The experimenter often uses the common dry cell (shown cut apart in Figure 9), consisting of a carbon rod, zinc can, and moist chemical filler. It is the interaction of these components that produces electricity. Electrons flow out of the terminal connected to the zinc and into the terminal connected to the carbon. A carbon-zinc dry cell has a voltage of 1.5 volts regardless of its size, whether it is our #6 cell, the familiar "D" cell, or a tiny "AAA" penlight cell. But the large #6 cell will deliver almost 75 times as much current as the penlight cell. In a fixed current application, such as keeping a flashlight bulb lit, the larger unit will do the job longer.

Many cells are connected together to produce higher-voltage bat-

FIGURE 10

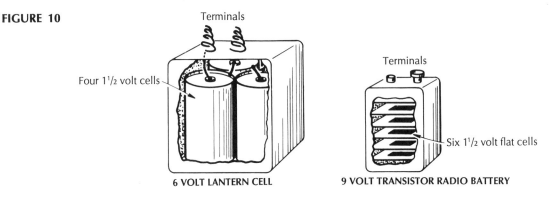

Multiple Cell Batteries

teries (Figure 10). In fact, the term "battery" really means two or more cells that have been connected together. A battery can be conveniently thought of as an electron pump, pushing electrons out of the cathode or negative (−) terminal and pulling electrons into the anode or positive (+) terminal.

Wet cell batteries such as the lead-acid battery used in automobiles (see the simplified form in Figure 11) are common. The electricity in such a battery is formed by the action of an acid-water

FIGURE 11

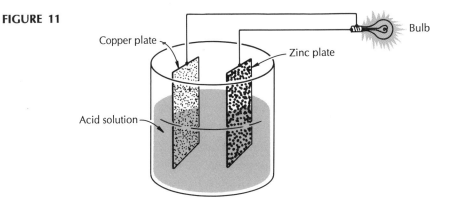

Simple "Wet" Cell

mixture on two plates, each made of a different metal. Other chemical batteries may use different metals, alkaline mixtures, and so on, but the common fault of all batteries remains: After a while the chemicals are used up to the point where voltage and current decrease and make the battery useless. This is why batteries are only useful for relatively short-lived applications, such as when current from a stationary source is unavailable.

Where continuous power is needed, as in homes, schools, and factories, the method used to produce electricity is based upon the fact that magnetic energy and electrical energy are easily converted to each other.

To illustrate this, we need a bar magnet of the kind supplied with some children's games and our current detector of Figure 2.

Referring to Figure 12, make a coil of 10 turns of ordinary bell wire approximately 1½- to 2-inches in diameter and connect it to the current detector. Now move the bar magnet quickly in and out of the "generator coil." The compass needle will deflect each time you move the magnet, proving that an electric current is flowing. The moving magnet is converting magnetic energy into electrical energy, which flows through the connecting wires to the detector. There, it is converted back into magnetic energy and deflects the compass needle.

If you were paying close attention, you noticed that when you

FIGURE 12

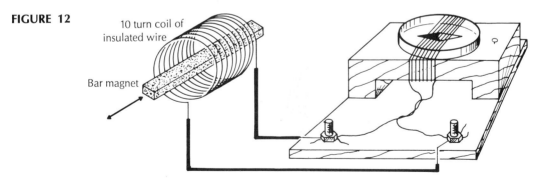

10 turn coil of insulated wire

Bar magnet

Generator Experiment

FIGURE 13

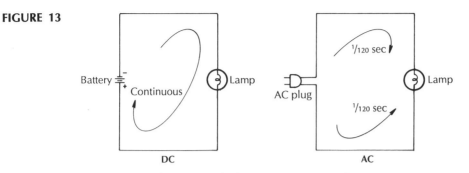

Comparison of Direct and Alternating Current Flow

moved the magnet into the coil, the compass deflected in one direction. When you pulled the magnet out of the coil, the needle moved in the opposite direction. What actually happened was that the current first flowed in one direction, then in the other. If a source of mechanical power was hooked up to move the magnet in and out of the coil continuously, the current that would be produced would reverse, or alternate, in the same manner. Such current is called an alternating current (or AC) and is the type that is supplied at the electrical outlets in our homes. Its direction of flow reverses at the rate of 120 times per second. Each back-and-forth electron motion is called a cycle. Utility companies in the United States supply 60 cycles per second AC, or simply 60 cycle AC. Current produced by a battery is called direct current (or DC), since the electrons flow only in one direction. Figure 13 summarizes both DC and AC current characteristics.

By means of other sources or power, such as water or steam, huge magnets are moved in close proximity to huge coils of wire, generating large amounts of alternating current in special generating stations owned and operated by the major electrical power companies. These generators operate as long as external mechanical power is applied to them. This is how we obtain the continuous electrical energy required by our society.

CHAPTER 3

SOURCES of electricity for the experimenter

To learn more about electricity we will, of course, have to perform many experiments, and all of these will require a source of electric current. We have already seen how the first battery was made and the principles behind the modern generator, but neither of these, in the forms described, will meet our needs. We require a source of DC and AC current that we can use (and abuse) with relative safety and one that will also supply adequate electric power for our projects.

There are two choices. One is common dry-cell batteries. The other is a low voltage version of the normal AC power line in our homes. Both of these will be discussed, and complete power sources, suitable for most experimental purposes, will be described. Also described will be a scheme to recharge, or at least extend the life of, exhausted batteries and, for those interested, a simple solar battery.

As we have already seen in Chapter 2, batteries come in all sizes and shapes. The one most suited for our needs is the #6, 1.5-volt "dry cell" unit. It has high current capability and can tolerate a good deal of electrical misuse. Such batteries can be obtained from most hardware stores, but they tend to be somewhat expensive, particularly for the experimenter on a limited budget. If cost is a factor, try visiting a local company that installs and services burglar alarms. Such companies use #6 batteries by the dozens and usually have a quantity of "slightly used" batteries available that will often be given to the experimenter who simply asks. In almost all cases these batteries have been removed from service for reliability purposes. They still have plenty of reserve capacity, however, and will suit the experimenter perfectly.

If you have not been able to obtain the batteries you require, common D cells can be used with good results, although they will become exhausted faster than larger ones.

The batteries we will be using all have an electrical pressure or potential of 1.5 volts. The current-producing capability, however, is a function of the size of the actual unit. Typical #6 dry cells can supply continuous currents of as high as 1.5 amperes, while D cells can only produce about one-tenth of that amount. Often higher voltages or currents will be required for particular experiments, so a bit of knowledge as to how batteries may be interconnected to achieve different voltages and currents is in order.

Since doing is preferable to a written explanation, we will learn how to vary voltage and current with a few simple experiments. To do these will require four #6 or D cells, some ordinary bell wire, a compass such as the one used in the current detector, and a 6-volt replacement lantern lamp with matching socket from the local hardware or electrical supplies store. The #6 cells have screw terminals for easy connections, but the D cells do not. If you are using D cells, four of the holders shown in Figure 14 must be built. These are simple and should pose no construction difficulties. After assembling the holders, drop a D cell into each, as shown, wedge it in place with cardboard, tighten the center screw, and you are ready to experiment. At this time it is advisable to test the holder by connecting a #222 flashlight lamp or other 1.5-volt lamp across the two terminal screws. If the lamp lights, the holder is functioning properly.

FIGURE 14

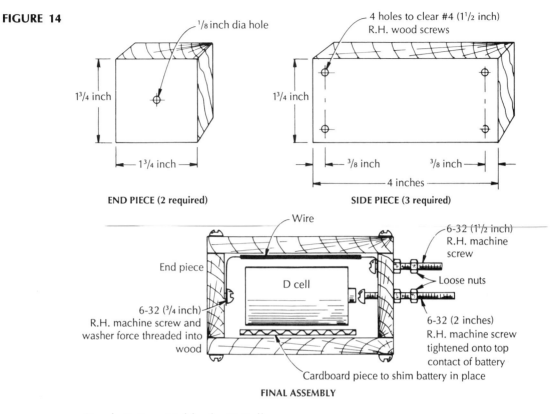

END PIECE (2 required)

SIDE PIECE (3 required)

FINAL ASSEMBLY

Simple Battery Holder for D Cells

Referring back to the water concept of Chapter 2, let us think of a battery as a tank of electrons under pressure, much like the liquid in a common aerosol can. The larger the can, the more liquid available (current capacity), but the pressure of the propelling gas (voltage) is the same regardless of size. A small can will therefore use up its contents quicker than a larger one even though the pressure is the same.

How then do we increase the current? Just add another can. Figure 15 shows how this is done with batteries and pressure cans. Such a connection is known as a parallel circuit. The two batteries are said to be in parallel, and the current capacity is now equal to the sum of the current capacities of each individual battery. To demonstrate this,

FIGURE 15

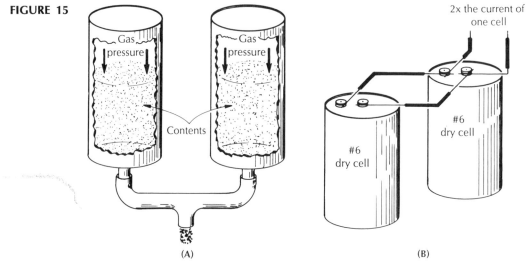

Connecting Batteries in Parallel

hook up the circuit shown in Figure 16. Turn the compass so that the needle is parallel to the wire and about 2 inches away from it. Now connect the free end of the wire to the battery just long enough to see how far the compass needle deflects. Move the compass closer or far-

FIGURE 16

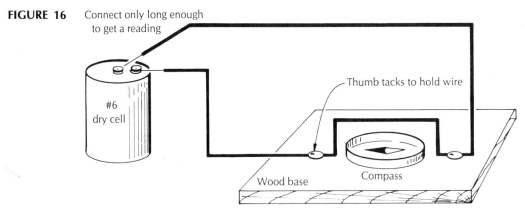

Current Measuring Experiment

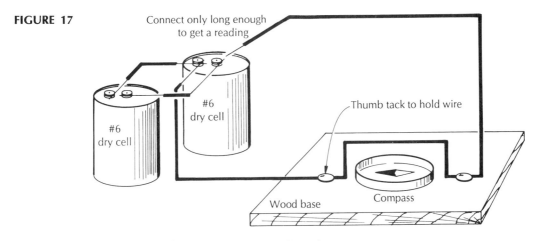

FIGURE 17

Connect only long enough to get a reading

#6 dry cell

#6 dry cell

Thumb tack to hold wire

Wood base

Compass

Completion of Current Measuring Experiment

ther away from the wire until the deflection is just enough to clearly see. A movement of about $\frac{1}{16}$ of an inch is fine. Now connect a second battery in parallel with the first and again connect the free wire to the battery. The compass needle will now deflect approximately twice as far, indicating the increased current capacity of the two batteries (Figure 17). Do not leave any of these circuits connected longer than necessary. The drain from the batteries is considerable and they will become exhausted in short order.

In a similar manner, you can increase the pressure or voltage of a group of batteries to enable more current to be pushed. This time, however, the batteries are connected in what is known as a series circuit. Figure 18 shows this configuration. To see the effect of such a circuit, first connect one battery to a #47, 6-volt lamp and notice how bright it is. Now connect a second battery, then a third, and finally the fourth. Notice how the lamp gets brighter each time the voltage increases. This increase is due to more and more current being pushed through the lamp. If you were to do the same experiment with parallel batteries, you would see that the lamp would remain at the same brightness regardless of how many batteries were added. Although in

FIGURE 18

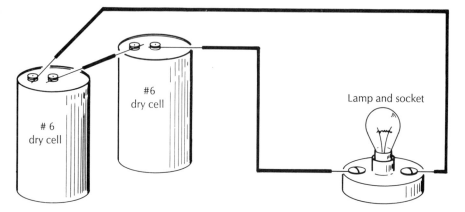

Series Connected Batteries

this case there is much more current available, there is not any more voltage to push it. Connect the batteries in parallel for more current capability and in series for more voltage.

Figure 19 is a drawing of an experimenter's DC power supply that will be of great convenience in future projects. It consists of four 1.5-volt batteries and a homemade switch allowing a selection of 1.5 through 6 volts to be achieved. The dimensions given will accommodate #6 dry cells; however, D cells can be used in the holders shown in Figure 14. The switch mechanism is made of tin can metal, and the

FIGURE 19

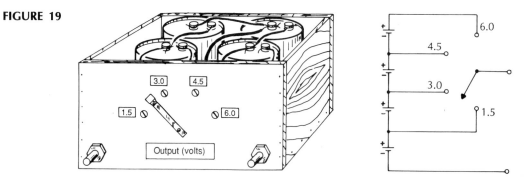

Experimenter's DC Power Supply

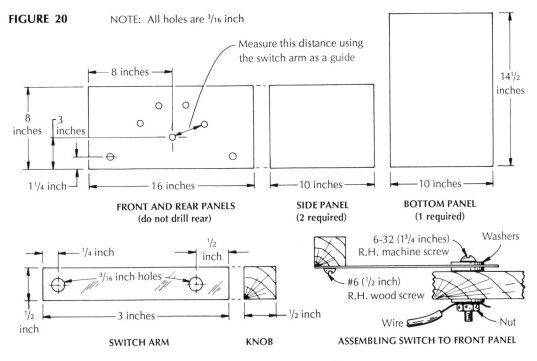

FIGURE 20 NOTE: All holes are ³/₁₆ inch

Measure this distance using the switch arm as a guide

8 inches

14¹/₂ inches

8 inches

3 inches

1¹/₄ inch

16 inches

10 inches

10 inches

FRONT AND REAR PANELS
(do not drill rear)

SIDE PANEL
(2 required)

BOTTOM PANEL
(1 required)

¹/₄ inch

¹/₂ inch

³/₁₆ inch holes

¹/₂ inch

3 inches

¹/₂ inch

¹/₂ inch

SWITCH ARM

KNOB

6-32 (1³/₄ inches)
R.H. machine screw

Washers

#6 (¹/₂ inch)
R.H. wood screw

Wire

Nut

ASSEMBLING SWITCH TO FRONT PANEL

Construction Details of the DC Power Supply

switch contacts are arranged so that an "off" position is present between each contact for standby purposes.

Begin by cutting all of the wood and drilling the holes as shown in Figure 20. Then cut the tin-can metal, file all sharp edges, and connect the wires as shown. Be sure all screws are tight and contacting surfaces are clean of paint, varnish, or other material that might act as an insulator. For appearances, the wood may be stained and varnished before assembly. *When cutting the tin-can metal, be sure to wear work gloves. The unfiled edges can be sharp and it is easy to get cut.*

Once the unit is built, it should be tested by connecting the #47, 6-volt lamp to the terminals. Moving the switch from one position to another should cause the lamp to get progressively brighter.

Producing AC for the experimenter is not much more complicated. Since generators are not easily built by experimenters, our power source will be derived from the household power line. To do this requires the use of a device called a transformer. As we have seen in the experiment of Figure 4, a changing electric current in a coil around an iron core will produce a changing magnetic field in the core. This magnetic field will then produce another changing current in a second coil wound around the same core. This is the principle of the transformer, and Figure 21 is a representation of the type of unit that is most common. It consists of two coils, wound over each other, on a core made of iron strips. The use of concentric coils and strips instead of a solid core is a modern day improvement for greater efficiency, but operation is exactly the same.

The coil that is the "input coil" is referred to as the primary and is designed to produce the proper strength magnetic field with the incoming current. The "output coil," or secondary, is wound with just enough wire to produce the current and voltage desired. The ratio of primary to secondary turns determines the actual transformation. For example, a transformer with a primary of 1000 turns of wire and a secondary of 100 turns of wire will convert a 100-volt input to a 10-volt output. The unit we will employ in our AC power supply will be a 115- to 6-volt commercial unit with a current capacity of 3 amperes.

FIGURE 21

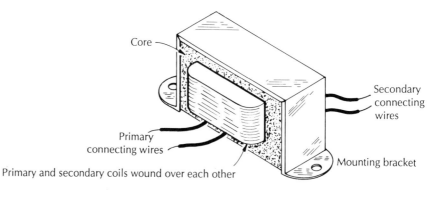

Parts of a Common Transformer

FIGURE 22

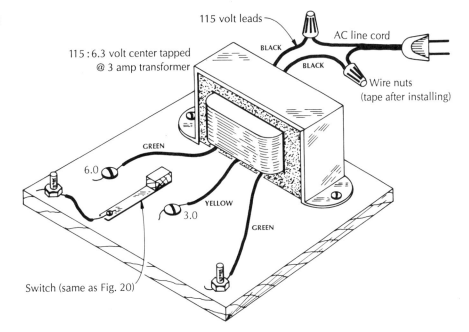

115 volt leads

AC line cord

BLACK

BLACK

115 : 6.3 volt center tapped
@ 3 amp transformer

Wire nuts
(tape after installing)

GREEN

6.0

YELLOW

3.0

GREEN

Switch (same as Fig. 20)

Construction Details of the AC Power Supply

This unit will supply all of the current required for our further experimentation.

Figure 22 shows the construction details of our AC power supply. The transformer can be obtained at most electronic parts suppliers and should be the type that has a "center tapped secondary." This feature allows both 6 volts and 3 volts to be obtained. (Note that the actual outputs are really 6.3 and 3.15 volts.) The switch, as in the DC supply, has a center position for "standby" use. When connecting the AC line cord to the primary of the transformer (the black wires), be absolutely certain that the connections are very well-insulated. After connecting the wires securely, thread wire nuts (from the hardware store) over the twisted ends and then use black vinyl electrical tape over the wire nuts. The 115-volt pressure of the AC power line is quite high and can push enough current through a person to cause serious injury or at least a bad shock. The transformer output is quite safe, however.

After completion, test the power source by connecting the 6-volt lamp to the terminals and moving the switch to its two positions. *As a safety precaution, always unplug the line cord when not using the AC supply.*

While the AC power source will operate indefinitely (as long as there is household AC power), batteries will not. Eventually the chemicals making up the individual cells will become used up and the battery will fail.

There is a way to try to extend the life of a normally nonrechargable 1.5-volt dry cell. This method is to force the chemical reaction to reverse by pushing current into the battery using our AC power source. While this method does not work with every weak battery, it is worth a try, as it will "rejuvenate" enough of them to be worthwhile.

To build the battery "rejuvenator" we will need two additional components, both readily available from the local electronics supplier. One is a 10-ohm ½-watt resistor and the other a 1N4002 silicon rectifier diode. The silicon rectifier diode will convert the AC current from our power source to DC current, and the resistor will limit the amount of current that can flow into the battery. Figure 23 shows the way these components are connected between the AC power source and the weak battery.

To test the effectiveness of the "rejuvenator," connect a weak

FIGURE 23

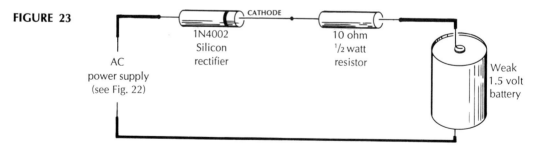

Battery Rejuvenator

1.5-volt dry cell to the circuit, set the AC power source to "6 volts," and allow everything to operate for 30 minutes. Now remove the battery and connect a #222 lamp across it to check on its condition. If the lamp does not light brightly, repeat the process for another 30 minutes. If after three repeated tries there is still no improvement, the battery cannot be saved and should be discarded.

As previously mentioned, this circuit will not work all of the time nor will it renew a dead battery. In addition, it should only be used with #6, D, or C type batteries. If at any time during the "rejuvenation" procedure the battery gets hot to the touch, immediately turn off the AC power source and discard the battery.

One source of DC power for the experimenter that deserves at least some mention is the solar battery. This device, shown in Figure 24, is very exciting in that it provides pure DC power when exposed to sunlight. Unfortunately the cost for a single solar cell is about $3 to $4 at this time, and three such cells are needed to provide the power of a D cell. Furthermore, for full power the cells must be in direct sunlight. The good part of all of this, however, is that they will continue to produce electric power almost indefinitely.

FIGURE 24

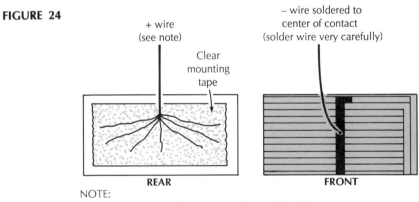

+ wire
(see note)

– wire soldered to
center of contact
(solder wire very carefully)

Clear
mounting
tape

REAR

FRONT

NOTE:
Wire must be taped in place, as it is very difficult to solder to the rear of the solar battery.

Solar Battery

FIGURE 25

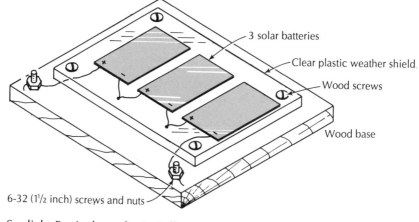

Sunlight Equivalent of a D Cell

As an optional experiment for those who wish to incur the cost, Figure 25 shows how to connect three common solar cells in series to produce the sunlight equivalent of a D cell or about 1.5 volts. Such an arrangement should be mounted in a sunny location and tested by means of a #222 lamp.

Solar batteries are currently used in large arrays to power remote telephone exchanges, small electronic equipment, and virtually all orbiting communications satellites around the earth.

CHAPTER 4

MEASURING ELECTRICITY

Sooner or later in one's pursuit of the mysteries of electricity, the need to measure voltage or current arises. Whether to check on the presence of current, the condition of a battery, or the continuity of a circuit, something beyond the simple "if-it-works-it's-okay" approach is needed.

Fortunately we have already fabricated two very useful devices—the tester of Figure 8 and the compass indicator of Figure 2. While neither of these will measure actual values, they will be found to be quite handy in our experimentation. While the tester of Figure 8 was originally intended to determine if something was an insulator or conductor, it will also be useful as a tester of switches, wire connections, or the general continuity of an electrical circuit. Likewise, the compass indicator is a sensitive detector of small amounts of current, much smaller than that produced by the batteries we employ in our experiments. But indicators are not enough. If serious work is to be done, we must have a way to actually measure voltage and current.

First, however, there is one electrical quantity in addition to voltage and current that we must understand, and this is resistance. We already know that voltage is required to push current through a circuit, but the amount of current that can be actually pushed is also a function of the circuit itself. Just like water pipes, large diameter wires will allow a great deal of current to flow while small, fine wires will only allow very little. The degree of opposition to electron conduction of any wire or complete electrical circuit is known as its resistance. Resistance is expressed in units called ohms in honor of Georg Simon Ohm, a German scientist of the early 1800s.

Ohm discovered a relationship between volts and amperes that has been the primary law or rule of electricity since serious work began. This rule is known as Ohm's Law. It states, very simply, that the resistance of a circuit is equal to the voltage applied to the circuit, divided by the resulting current that flows. In simple mathematical terms, $R = V/I$. A lamp that has 6 volts applied and uses 2 amperes to light up has a resistance, therefore, of 3 ohms. If you reduce the voltage to 3 volts, then only 1 ampere will flow. Resistance is a constant factor as long as the temperature remains unchanged. By rearranging the relationship of V, I, and R, any one of the factors or parameters may be determined if you know the other two. For example $V = I \times R$, and $I = V/R$. Now, if you know the resistance of a circuit, you can accurately predict what will happen if you increase or decrease either voltage or current.

Figure 26 shows a typical low-cost commercially manufactured electrical multimeter of the type that should be acquired by any experimenter whose interest in electricity goes beyond simple "tinkering." Usually available at a cost of $10 and up, meters such as the one shown will allow voltage, current, and resistance to be measured with accuracies that are more than adequate for the experimenter.

A typical multimeter, or V-O-M as it is often called (for volts-ohms-milliamperes), has a large meter with a number of scales, a main selector switch, and one or two other adjustments, depending on the style of the meter. The selector switch allows the main meter to be

FIGURE 26

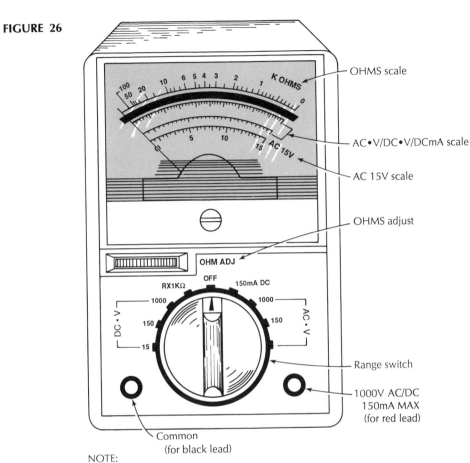

OHMS scale

AC•V/DC•V/DCmA scale

AC 15V scale

OHMS adjust

Range switch

1000V AC/DC
150mA MAX
(for red lead)

Common
(for black lead)

NOTE:
 The *red lead* goes to the most positive point in the circuit.

A Typical Low-Cost Multimeter

switched to measure DC or AC volts, DC current, and resistance in several overlapping ranges. V-O-Ms are also supplied with a set of test probes to make actual connections to the circuit being tested.

While using a V-O-M is quite easy, there are a number of pointers one can learn from the professionals that will make the procedure run more smoothly.

When measuring AC or DC voltage, even though you know the approximate voltage in the circuit, always start by setting the selector switch to its highest range. If we were to measure the output voltage of two D cells in series (approximately 3 volts), for example, we would set the meter to the 1000 volt DC range. When the tiny deflection of the meter pointer was noted, we would change to the 150-volt range. If we still did not get enough deflection, we would finally change to the 15-volt range and make our measurement. This procedure has one very important benefit. You do not damage or "blow out" an expensive meter because what you thought was 3 volts really turned out to be 30 volts due to a problem in the circuit. When measuring voltage, the two test probes are always connected across (or in parallel with) the item whose voltage or voltage drop is to be measured. Figure 27 shows where the voltage measurement across the battery and across the lamp would be made in a simple flashlight.

When measuring current, the same procedure with regard to range switching applies. Some V-O-Ms have only one switch-selected current range but a separate test probe connecter for the higher current ranges. You should become familiar with the way your meter works by thoroughly reading the instruction manual that comes with it.

When measuring current, the meter is connected in series at the point where the current measurement is desired, so that the full current

FIGURE 27

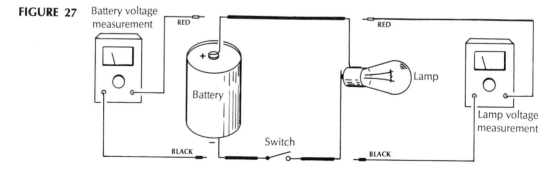

Voltage Measurements in a Simple Flashlight

FIGURE 28

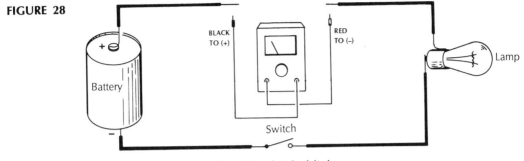

BLACK
TO (+)

RED
TO (−)

Lamp

Battery

Switch

Current Measurements in a Simple Flashlight

runs through the meter. Figure 28 shows how the current of the flash-light would be measured. A V-O-M has two connecting wires or leads, each color-coded. Red stands for positive (+) while black stands for negative (−). When using a V-O-M to measure DC current or voltage, the positive lead (+) is always connected so that it runs directly or ultimately to the (+) terminal of the power supply. Of course, the negative lead (−) connects so that it ultimately leads to the (−) termi-nal of the supply. Note how this is done in Figure 27 and Figure 28. A good habit to develop is this: Watch your V-O-M pointer-needle just as you make connection. If the needle moves the wrong way, *instantly* break the connection and check the circuit. Doing this will avoid "burning out" the delicate meter movement.

It should be noted here that the electrical currents encountered in the majority of circuits that use batteries of the D size and smaller rarely exceed 1 ampere. As a result, most V-O-Ms have milliampere current ranges. One milliampere is $\frac{1}{1000}$ of an ampere, so 250 milli-amperes is $\frac{1}{4}$ of an ampere, 500 milliamperes is $\frac{1}{2}$ ampere, and so forth. In the case where currents higher than the ranges of the meter need to be measured, the voltage and resistance should first be mea-sured and the current calculated using Ohm's Law (I = V/R).

Resistance is measured a little differently. When using a V-O-M on its resistance ranges, *never have power applied to the circuit— never!* To do so will almost certainly damage the meter or blow any internal fuse. The actual measurement is done in two parts. First the test probes are touched to each other (which is the equivalent of zero ohms). All V-O-Ms have a zero adjustment, which is usually a regular knob or thumbwheel type control labeled "zero adjust," "ohms adjust," or something similar. This adjustment is now turned until the meter pointer indicates zero ohms. Notice that the ohms scale reads backwards from the voltage or current scales. After "zeroing the meter," the test probes are connected across (in parallel with) the points to be measured and the resistance read on the scale. If the reading is at either extreme end of the ohms scale, the meter should be re-zeroed on another range and the measurement repeated. Most resistance ranges are signified by a multiplier such as R × 10. This means that when on the R × 10 range, any reading should be multiplied by 10. A reading of 50 on that range, therefore, signifies 500 ohms.

In conclusion, all V-O-Ms have an off position. Since they all contain internal batteries for the ohms ranges, when they are not in use they should be turned off. It is usually quite common for the newcomer to go through several sets of batteries before this procedure becomes a habit.

CHAPTER 5

TOOLS OF THE TRADE

At this point, the future experimenter will be starting to understand what electricity is all about. Voltage, current, resistance, circuits, etc., should no longer be strange words. We are therefore ready to look at the components and tools that will be used to build, modify, and repair our working models.

Aside from the battery or other source of electricity, the most common item is, of course, the connecting wires. We already know that the larger the diameter of a wire, the more current it can accommodate, which is why electrical wire is manufactured in a wide range of sizes. Figure 29 shows some of the sizes likely to be encountered and the maximum current they will handle safely. All common electrical wire is manufactured of copper and is covered with a nonconducting coating referred to as insulation. The insulation prevents the loss of current if the wires come in contact with other bodies or themselves. Insulation is made of a wide range of materials that are in-

FIGURE 29

WIRE SIZE	DIAMETER OF CONDUCTOR (INCHES)	MAXIMUM ALLOWABLE CURRENT (AMPERES)	TYPICAL USE
#10	.102	32.5	
#12	.081	23.0	General house wiring
#14	.064	16.2	
#16	.051	11.5	Bells, buzzers, appliances
#18	.040	8.1	
#20	.036	5.5	
#22	.025	4.0	Electronic wiring
#24	.020	2.0	
#26	.016	–	
#28	.013	–	Transformers
#30	.010	–	

Typical Wires and Important Specifications

tended for specific applications. Wires used for appliance power cords, for example, may be covered with rubber or plastic material for flexibility, whereas those used within the walls of houses have heavy, nonflammable plastic coatings. Underground wires often have similar plastic insulation that is further enclosed in lead or other metallic outer jackets. Wires intended for high temperature use are usually insulated with ceramic beads or mica holders, while those intended for underwater use have heavy rubber coatings. The wire that the experimenter will find most convenient for his or her use will almost always have either a plastic insulation or a thin enamel coating and will have a solid or stranded copper conductor. The stranded wire is made to obtain greater flexibility—especially in the larger diameter conductors—and for most purposes is interchangeable with the solid type. Figure 30 shows some of the types of wire in use today.

Now that the circuit can be interconnected, we want to be able to easily turn it on and off. This is the function of the switch. Very simply stated, a switch either makes or breaks a circuit. The operation of the common knife switch, shown in Figure 31 and available in most hardware stores, is obvious, and all switches—whether rotary, toggle, slide, or pushbutton—work in the same manner. Either there is a complete electrical path through them or there is not. Figure 32 shows

FIGURE 30

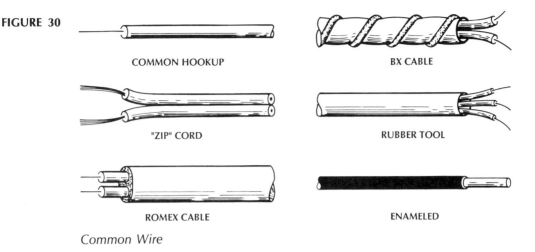

COMMON HOOKUP

BX CABLE

"ZIP" CORD

RUBBER TOOL

ROMEX CABLE

ENAMELED

Common Wire

several switches that can be made of wood, screws, and tin can metal. All of these are suitable for use with the 6-volt DC or AC power supplies of Chapter 3. *They should not be used directly with the AC power line, as serious shocks may result!*

There are a number of methods suggested for connecting wires to each other or to other parts of a circuit. These are shown in Figure 33. When using methods (A) and (B), remove only enough insulation from

FIGURE 31

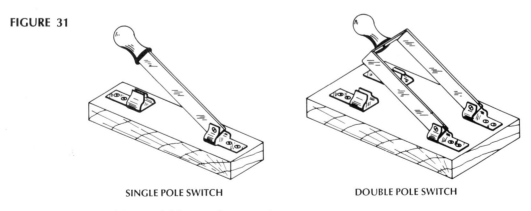

SINGLE POLE SWITCH

DOUBLE POLE SWITCH

Readily Available "Knife" Switches

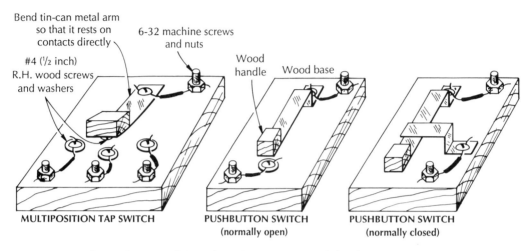

Bend tin-can metal arm so that it rests on contacts directly

#4 (½ inch) R.H. wood screws and washers

6-32 machine screws and nuts

Wood handle

Wood base

MULTIPOSITION TAP SWITCH

PUSHBUTTON SWITCH (normally open)

PUSHBUTTON SWITCH (normally closed)

FIGURE 32 *Several Types of Switches That Can Be Built by the Experimenter*

the wire for the "twist." Then wrap plastic or vinyl electrical tape over the connection until no bare metal shows through. When using "wire nuts" (C), be sure they are the right size for the wire you are using. The

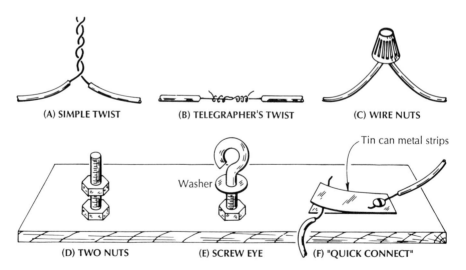

(A) SIMPLE TWIST

(B) TELEGRAPHER'S TWIST

(C) WIRE NUTS

Washer

Tin can metal strips

(D) TWO NUTS

(E) SCREW EYE

(F) "QUICK CONNECT"

FIGURE 33 *Several Methods of Joining Wires*

binding posts of Figure 33(D) and (E) are self-explanatory. They should always be securely tightened to make a good connection. The assembly shown in Figure 33(F) is a "quick connect" post made of tin can metal that will be useful for temporary hookups. In use a wire is simply slid between the two metal strips. It should be clearly understood that the object of all of the methods shown in Figure 33 is to assure good metallic contact between all of the conductors involved. Be sure that there is no coating on the metal strips of the "quick connect" post.

To assure even better contact between connecting wires and other components, most electrical connections are soldered. Soldering is a skill that is easily learned and perfected by practice. To start, drive a small brass brad or nail into a block of wood as shown in Figure 34. Wrap two wires around the nail as shown, being sure that the wires have no insulation or coating where they touch each other or the nail. Heat the nail and wires with a pencil-type soldering iron (30 to 50 watts). A higher wattage iron is unnecessary. After 4 to 5 seconds, touch the heated joint with 60-40 rosin core solder until a small quantity of the solder melts and flows over the points to be connected. This should not take more than 5 seconds. Do not overdo it; use solder sparingly. Beginners often use too much solder or don't allow enough

FIGURE 34

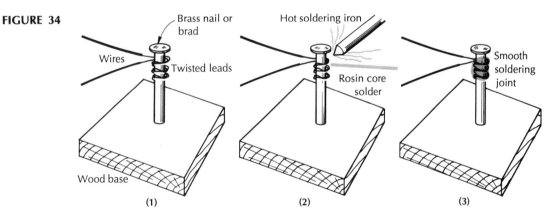

Steps in Soldering

FIGURE 35

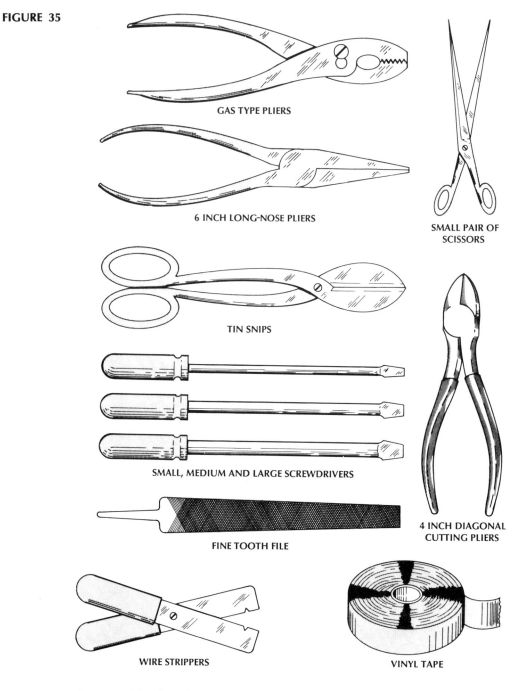

GAS TYPE PLIERS

6 INCH LONG-NOSE PLIERS

SMALL PAIR OF
SCISSORS

TIN SNIPS

SMALL, MEDIUM AND LARGE SCREWDRIVERS

4 INCH DIAGONAL
CUTTING PLIERS

FINE TOOTH FILE

WIRE STRIPPERS

VINYL TAPE

Common Hand Tools

time to heat the connections properly. Try to get an experienced solderer to help you learn. With correct guidance it will not take more than 15 minutes. If you plan extensive electrical experimentation, soldering is a skill that you must master. *Never use solder other than rosin core. It will corrode and ruin your project!*

General electrical experimentation will be made much easier and more enjoyable if the experimenter obtains some basic hand tools. These tools need not be expensive but should be of the best quality one can afford so they will give long, reliable service—particularly with heavy usage.

If at all possible, the experimenter's tool complement should include:

1. Three slotted screwdrivers, one for use with #12 through ¼-inch screws, one for use with #6 through #10 screws, and a fine blade screwdriver for use with #4 or smaller screws
2. A pair of gas type pliers
3. A pair of 6-inch long-nose pliers
4. A pair of 4-inch diagonal cutting pliers
5. A pair of wire strippers
6. A small pair of scissors
7. A 6- to 8-inch fine-tooth file
8. An inexpensive pair of tin snips
9. A roll of black vinyl electrical tape

Figure 35 shows some examples of the type of tools that you should try to obtain. Optional items such as woodworking tools, a hand drill, and so on can be added as needed.

CHAPTER 6

solid-state devices and transistors

At this point, the experimenter should be well aware of the characteristics of electrical conductors and insulators. Most metals are conductors and pass electrical current easily. Materials such as glass, plastic, wood, mica, etc., are insulators and do not.

There is a group of materials, however, that are neither good conductors nor good insulators. Most of these semiconductors, as they are called, are not particularly exciting as far as electricity is concerned, but certain ones, notably silicon and germanium, are the basis of our solid-state industry.

In the early days of radio communications, just after the beginning of the twentieth century, scientists found that certain materials, such as iron pyrites, commonly known as "fool's gold," quartz, and certain oxidized metal surfaces, had the strange property of allowing an electrical current to easily flow in one direction but not in the other. These "crystals" were initially used to detect feeble radio waves. Their one-way conducting feature made them ideal for converting alternating current to direct current, however, and the solid-state, semiconductor rectifier was born.

You will remember, from Chapter 2 and Figure 13, that an AC current changes its direction of flow many times per second while a DC current always flows in one direction. By connecting a semiconductor rectifier in series with a wire that normally has an AC current flowing, one direction of flow will be uninterrupted while the other will be stopped. The AC will be converted to a sort of interrupted or pulsed DC.

Solid-state rectifiers, or diodes as they are commonly called, come in all sizes and shapes, from the small device we have used to huge units that can handle the output of power plants that serve cities. Figure 36 shows what some of these look like. While solid-state diodes are useful for changing AC to DC, they also have interesting possibilities in signaling circuits like the one in Figure 37. Here, two switches control two lamps totally independent of one another, but over one connecting wire. By tracing the circuit of each switch/diode/lamp it is easy to see that counterclockwise interrupted DC current flows through S1, D1, D2, and L1 when S1 is closed. Clockwise interrupted DC current flows through S2, D3, D4, and L2, when S2 is closed. Neither interferes with the other, and S1 controls only L1, S2, only L2. To perform the same function without solid-state diodes would take the circuit of Figure 38 and one additional wire. It is interesting to actually hook up Figure 37; all that it requires is two 1N4002 rectifier diodes, two #47, 6-volt lamps, two switches, and the

FIGURE 36

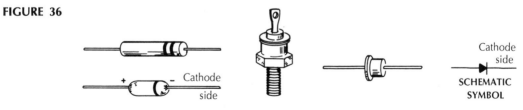

Solid-State Rectifier Diodes

FIGURE 37

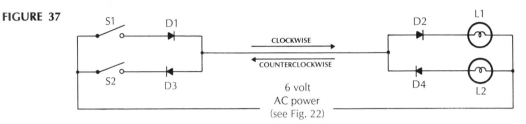

Two Switches Control Two Lamps

AC power source of Figure 22, set to 6 volts output. It should be noted that while 2 lamps can be controlled by 2 wires (instead of 3, as in Figure 39), 10 lamps could be controlled by 6 wires instead of 11.

Semiconductor diodes can also be used to "route" DC voltages in signaling circuits. Figure 40 shows a five-section alert system that will light one of five lamps corresponding to one of five buttons pressed, as well as a common buzzer for both visual and audible signaling. The diodes allow the individual lamps to light only when the respective button is pressed, while the buzzer sounds when any button is pressed. Tracing the circuit shows how the reverse blocking action of the diode prevents adjacent lamps from lighting at the wrong time. This will operate on 6-volt DC or AC.

Rectifiers and diodes were the extent of the solid-state industry until 1948. In that year, scientists at the Bell Telephone Laboratories in New Jersey found that by modifying the way a diode was manufactured, they could cause it not only to rectify but to act as a switch and to amplify an electrical current as well. The transistor was born!

To understand how the transistor operates, we must first take a

FIGURE 38

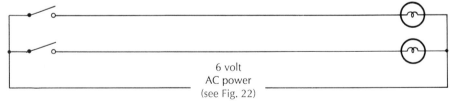

Two Switches Control Two Lamps without Diodes

FIGURE 39

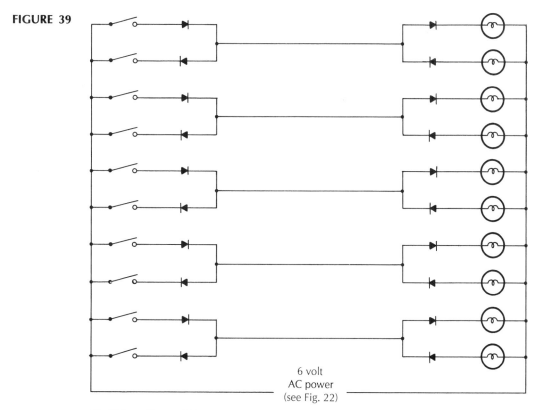

6 volt
AC power
(see Fig. 22)

Six Wires Control Ten Lamps

quick look at electrical amplification and switching. Figure 41 is a drawing of an electromechanical device called a relay. As is apparent from the drawing, the relay consists of an electromagnet, wound with many turns of wire, and a set of contacts that are activated by the pull of the electromagnet. As shown in Figure 42, a current flowing through the electromagnet in one circuit switches the current flowing through the contacts in the other circuit. Furthermore, the coil is usually wound so that a small current through it can activate contacts that are capable of handling a very large current. In an automobile starter relay, for example, a small 2–3-ampere current from the ignition switch controls a hundred or more amperes to start the car.

FIGURE 40

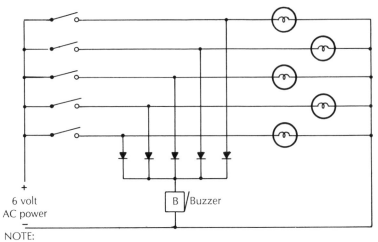

NOTE:
   If 6 volt DC is used, connect to (+) and (−) terminals of battery as shown.

Alarm System

   The transistor is, in some ways, the solid state equivalent of the relay. A typical transistor (Figure 43) consists of a tiny bar of silicon or germanium that has been treated so that three distinct regions—the emitter, base, and collector—have been formed. Without going into a long technical discussion, we can say that the main current flows between the collector and emitter. This current is controlled by a much smaller current flowing between the base and emitter. Since collector

FIGURE 41

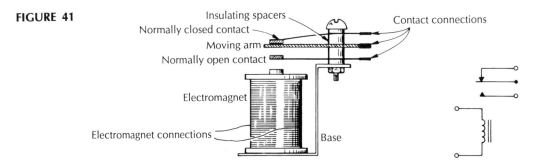

A Typical Electromagnetic Relay

FIGURE 42

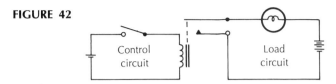

The Circuit of a Relay

current is many times base current, amplification occurs. In addition, with zero base current, zero collector current flows, so that the device is also an effective switch.

While most transistors operate at less than 12 volts and at currents in the milliampere range, there are power devices that will handle thousands of volts and thousands of amperes. Transistors are also very small. The actual transistor element is so tiny that you would need a microscope to see it. Hundreds, even thousands of transistors are often packed in thumbnail size modules known as integrated circuits. These integrated circuits (or ICs) are, for the most part, complete functional building blocks such as amplifiers, computer logic elements, industrial control devices, and electronic sensors. No matter how complex the integrated circuit, however, it is still made up of individual components—but very small ones. Figure 44 shows what commonly available transistors and integrated circuits look like and what the schematic diagram symbol for a transistor is.

To see how a transistor works, we will need our V-O-M, a #47 6-volt lamp, our 6-volt DC power supply (Figure 19), a 1N4002 silicon diode, a medium power general purpose NPN transistor, type 2N3053

FIGURE 43

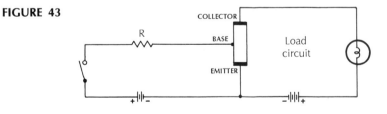

The Transistor and a Common Circuit

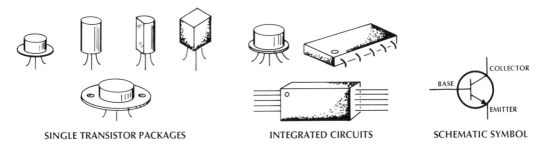

SINGLE TRANSISTOR PACKAGES   INTEGRATED CIRCUITS   SCHEMATIC SYMBOL

FIGURE 44   *Transistors and Integrated Circuits*

or equivalent, and a 470-ohm carbon resistor. The last two items are available from most electronic parts suppliers and should cost less than $2.00.

To begin, connect the lamp, silicon diode, V-O-M, and power supply (set to 4.5 volts) as shown in Figure 45. The diode is used to simulate the dropping voltage that will occur when the transistor is used in the next part of this experiment. Notice that it requires about 100 milliamperes to light the lamp. Now connect the transistor in place of the diode as shown in Figure 46. With the base of the transistor left unconnected, no current flows and the lamp does not light. Connect the base via the 470-ohm resistor as shown, and the lamp again lights. From Figure 45, you know that it requires about 100-milliamperes to light the lamp. Notice how much less current is needed by the base circuit to switch the transistor. It is interesting to note that this type of circuit is quite common in industry where it is

FIGURE 45

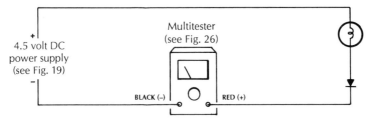

4.5 volt DC power supply (see Fig. 19)

Multitester (see Fig. 26)

BLACK (–)   RED (+)

Part 1 of Transistor Experiment

FIGURE 46

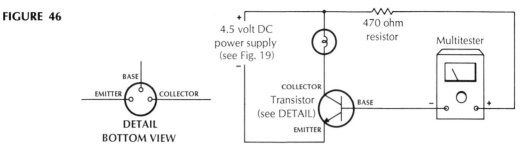

Part 2 of Transistor Experiment

employed to control lamps, motors, electromagnetic devices and a wide range of similar "on-off" type devices. Unlike the relay, a transistor can switch at speeds in excess of many millions of times per second. Also, there are no mechanical contacts, bearings, or springs to wear out.

CHAPTER 7

ELECTRICAL SENSORS

Although we take them for granted, some of the wonders of our technology, such as doors that open automatically as we approach them, thermostats that regulate the temperature of our homes in both summer and winter, and lights that come on as the sun sets, are really quite amazing but simple in principle. Furthermore, many are easily duplicated by the experimenter.

At the heart of much of this technology is a device called a sensor. It is the job of this sensor to react to some outside stimulus such as light, heat, temperature, or position, etc., and then control the flow of an electrical current so that some action occurs.

The turning on of a heater when the room gets too cold, the sounding of an alarm when someone goes into a restricted area, or the turning on of a pump when a basement floods, are all actions initiated by sensors.

Sensors come in two basic types: analog and digital. Analog sensors continuously vary the amount of current flowing in a circuit, while digital sensors simply switch the current on and off. Since digital sensors are easy to build and use, the ones we build in this chapter will be digital. The following sensor example, however, will be analog so that we at least have a bit of an understanding of this type.

In Chapter 3, we explored the use of solar batteries as a source of electrical power. The individual solar cell, however, also makes an excellent light sensor. To see how such a sensor works, connect your solar cell to a sensitive current range of your V-O-M as in Figure 47. Place a table lamp with a 25-watt bulb about 24 inches away from the cell and turn on the lamp. Note the reading on the V-O-M. Now change the bulb to 40 watts, 60 watts, and finally, 100 watts. Notice the change in current produced by the cell. Since the amount of current produced by such a sensor is directly related to the amount of light present, it is an analog sensor.

With a little bit of effort, the solar cell can be converted into a light-sensitive relay that can be the basis of many interesting and unique applications. Figure 48 shows the schematic diagram of the circuit and Figure 49 shows the details. The relay is a single pole double throw unit with a 5-volt 100-ohm (or higher) coil. Suitable types are available at most electronic parts suppliers for a few dollars. When light strikes the solar cell, an electron current is produced that flows through the 100-ohm resistor and base to emitter path of the transistor.

FIGURE 47

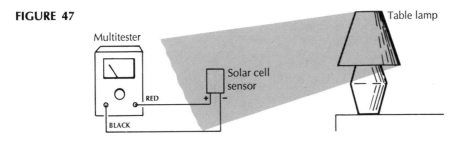

Analog Sensor Experiment

49

FIGURE 48

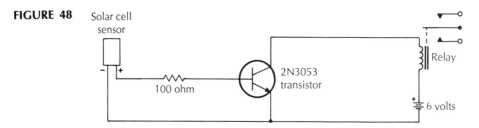

A Light-Sensitive Relay

This current causes the collector to emitter path to conduct, and the relay closes. The relay's contacts can then be wired to switch an external circuit.

The light sensor is mounted at the end of a cardboard tube such as the ones paper towels or aluminum foil comes on. This tube acts as a baffle and controls the area that the light sensor "sees." With a 12-inch long tube, the "seeing area" is small. By shortening the tube, you

FIGURE 49

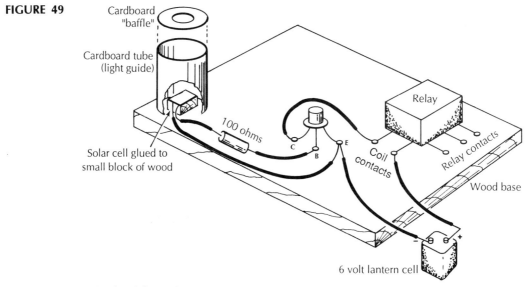

Details of the Light-Sensitive Relay

can widen this area. To get some idea of just what this area is, simply look through the tube before you mount it to the solar cell. If you wish to vary the sensitivity of the circuit, fit the open end of the tube with a cardboard disk that has a hole cut in the center of it. The size of this hole determines how much light will pass and, therefore, the sensitivity of the circuit. For best results, paint the inside of the tube with flat black paint.

The light sensor will make an excellent sunlight detector. By connecting a table lamp to it as shown in Figure 50, you can have light whenever the sun goes down. *If you build this circuit, be sure the relay contacts can handle the 115-volt AC line and that you fully insulate and do not come in contact with any part of the circuit that is connected to the AC line.* AN INADVERTENT SHOCK FROM THE AC LINE CAN BE DANGEROUS AND, IN SOME CASES, FATAL, SO USE EXTREME CARE!

If you arrange a narrow beam spotlight to shine on the light sensor as in Figure 51, you have a simple intrusion detector. Any person "breaking the beam" will be detected. Finally, by using a flashlight with a push button as a "gun," a simple shooting gallery can be constructed. The uses are limited only by one's imagination.

Temperature is a variable factor parameter, like light, that is analog in nature. The simplest and most widely used sensor for tem-

FIGURE 50

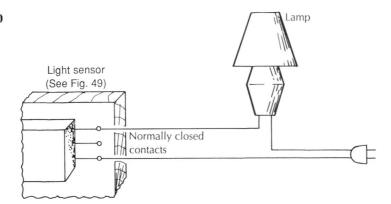

An Automatic Night Light

FIGURE 51

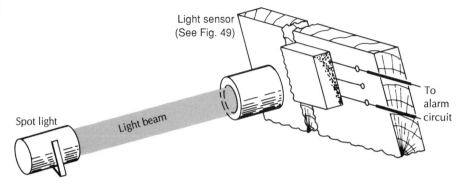

A Simple Intrusion Detector

perature is the thermostat. This sensor, however, is digital in nature. Thermostats are employed in devices that range all the way from home heating and air-conditioning systems to electric coffee pots. In most instances, the thermostat responds to some preset temperature and then turns a heater or cooler on and off. Figure 52 is a circuit diagram of a simple room heater. When the temperature drops below some preset point, the thermostat contacts close and the heater and fan connected in parallel blow warm air into the room. When the temperature rises, the contacts open and the process stops.

The heart of the thermostat is a thin strip of two different metals, usually brass and steel, tightly bonded together as shown in Figure 53. This bi-metallic strip has the unique property of bending when the temperature changes. The reason for this is that all metals expand or contract as a function of temperature. When metals with widely vary-

FIGURE 52

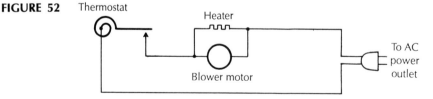

A Thermostat-Controlled Room Heater

FIGURE 53

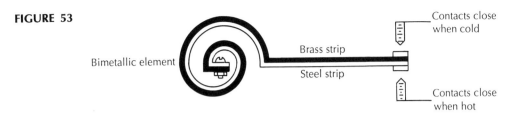

A Typical Thermostat

ing expansion rates are locked together, the one with the greater expansion rate tends to "curl" around the other and the strip bends. The drawing also shows how contacts are arranged to take advantage of this bending and produce a complete temperature sensitive switch.

The experimenter can fabricate a usable thermostat for temperature control experiments quite easily. What is needed is a thin strip of brass and one of steel, cut to the size shown in Figure 54. A

FIGURE 54

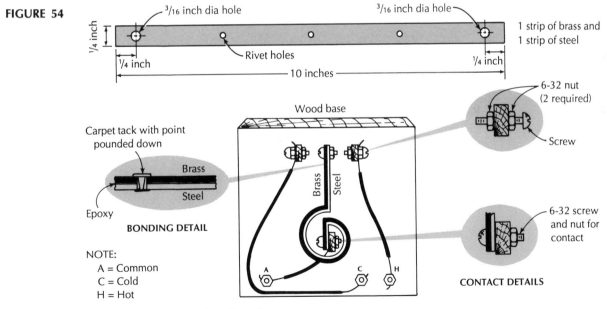

Thermostat Construction Details

good source for the steel is a "tin" can. (Check it with a magnet to be sure it really is steel.) The brass can be obtained from a hardware store in the form of so-called "shim stock." The thickness should match the steel and should be about 0.003 to 0.005 inches thick. Bond the strips together with a good quality adhesive, such as epoxy resin, and a couple of "rivets" made from carpet tacks. This operation is also shown in Figure 54.

The surfaces to be bonded should be cleaned with sandpaper before gluing and the carpet tacks pounded flat with a hammer. The screws used for the electrical contacts must also make good electrical contact to the strip.

When the bi-metallic strip is finished, bend it to the shape shown and mount it to the wooden holder. The exact amount of temperature "sensitivity" of the strip has to be determined next. With everything mounted, place a small index card on the wooden base just under the bi-metallic strip. Mark the orientation of the strip on the card with a pencil. Now run a hair blower, at full heat, over the strip for a moment and note the deflection. The strip should tend to move in the direction of the steel since brass expands faster than steel.

To set the thermostat to trigger at a particular temperature, place a thermometer as close to the strip as possible without actually touching. Heat or cool the unit (hair blower, refrigerator, etc.) until the proper temperature is obtained. Now adjust the proper contact screw until it just touches the strip. Be certain you adjust the screw on the brass side for cold and the one on the steel side for heat. Figure 55 shows two

FIGURE 55

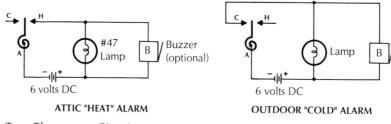

ATTIC "HEAT" ALARM   OUTDOOR "COLD" ALARM

Two Thermostat Circuits

FIGURE 56

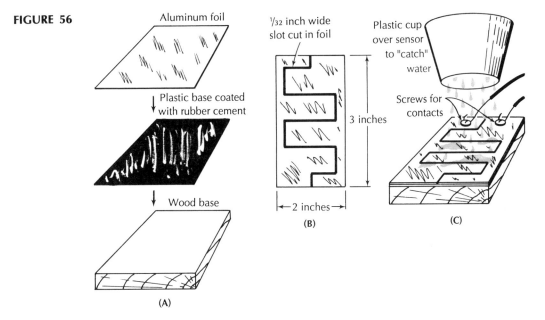

Aluminum foil

Plastic base coated with rubber cement

Wood base

(A)

¹/₃₂ inch wide slot cut in foil

3 inches

2 inches

(B)

Plastic cup over sensor to "catch" water

Screws for contacts

(C)

Construction Details of a Water Sensor

circuits that can be used with the homemade thermostat. If fabricated and adjusted carefully, it can be sensitive enough to respond to changes of a degree or so.

Construction details for a moisture sensor that can be used to detect rain, a flooding basement, or any other water leak are given in Figure 56. This sensor is made by first gluing a piece of aluminum foil onto an insulating base such as a wood or plastic plate. When the glue dries, the pattern shown in the drawing should be cut with a sharp hobby knife and the foil between the cuts carefully removed. Finally, a plastic drinking cup with the bottom removed should be glued over the cut area to complete the sensor. The circuit of Figure 57 is then connected to act as a sensitive detector of the small current that will flow when water falls on the gap in the sensor. Test the sensor with tap water. In the event that more sensitivity is needed, a pinch of table salt can be sprinkled lightly on the gap. Dry salt will not conduct. When

FIGURE 57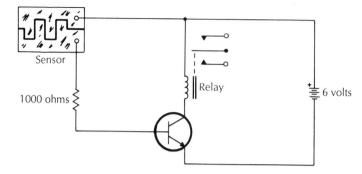

Sensor

1000 ohms

Relay

6 volts

Electrical Circuit of Water Sensor

mixed with water, however, it will produce a solution that will readily conduct.

A sensor that is very easy to build is shown with its appropriate circuit in Figure 58. This sensor is nothing more than a length of solder that has been flattened and connected in a simple series circuit. Since solder melts at a relatively low temperature, it can be used as the basis of a simple fire alarm. In the circuit shown, should any solder loop melt, the transistor will conduct, the relay will pull in and actuate any buzzer or lamp connected to it.

Last but not least, a readily available 115-volt AC relay can be employed as a simple power failure alarm. The coil of the relay is

FIGURE 58

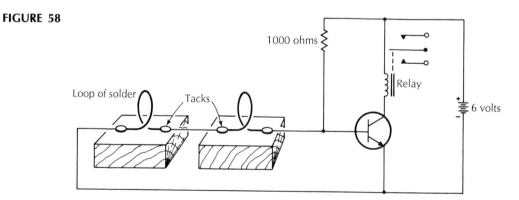

1000 ohms

Relay

6 volts

Loop of solder

Tacks

A Simple Fire Alarm

wired to a line cord and plug and the normally closed contacts are wired to an alarm circuit, as in the previous example. The relay is then plugged into an outlet that has an appliance such as a refrigerator or freezer also connected. If power fails, the relay will open, its contacts close, and the alarm sound. Since there is no current drawn in the alarm circuit until the relay actually opens, battery life will be extremely long.

IF YOU BUILD THIS CIRCUIT, OR ANY OTHER CIRCUIT THAT USES THE AC LINE IN ANY MANNER WHATSOEVER, USE EXTREME CAUTION. CHECK ALL CONNECTIONS THREE TIMES BEFORE APPLYING POWER AND PARTICULARLY CHECK TO SEE THAT THERE ARE NO EXPOSED CONTACTS, CONNECTIONS, OR WIRES. A SHOCK FROM THE AC POWER LINE CAN BE FATAL.

After building some of the sensors in this chapter, the experimenter will have an understanding of the way many of the common sensors of industry operate. These examples should stimulate the development of new sensors to meet the experimenter's specific needs.

CHAPTER 8

A PRACTICAL WEATHER STATION FOR THE EXPERIMENTER

By utilizing some of the techniques described in previous chapters, the experimenter can build a respectable weather station that can be used to learn about predicting and analyzing weather patterns.

The weather station to be described will permit the measurement of wind direction, wind speed, amount of rainfall, temperature, and sunlight intensity. The equipment will take the form of an indoor "display unit" and several outdoor "remote units." The complete station has been designed to be built in stages. Depending on the budget of the experimenter, a few or all of the instruments can be constructed at any one time.

Figure 59 shows construction details of the wind direction monitor. As can be seen from the drawing, it is simply an "electrified" weather vane. The basic vane itself is built from either flattened tin can metal or thin masonite that has been given a couple of coats of varnish to make it weather resistant. The wooden dowels are also treated with

FIGURE 59

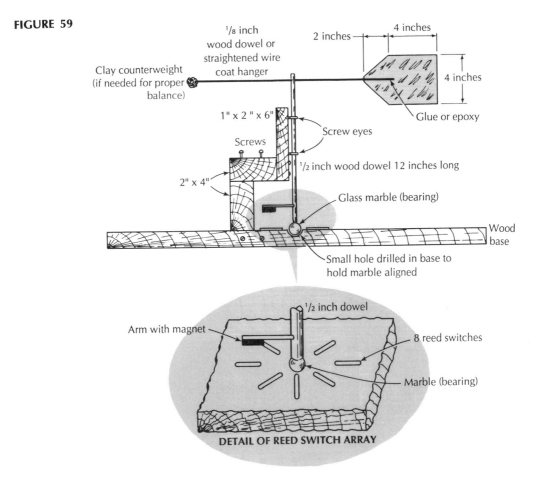

Construction Details of Wind Direction Indicator

varnish for the same reason. The screw-eye and marble bearing assembly is fairly simple to build and align, and the only effort is to get the assembly balanced so that it turns freely. What requires a bit of adjustment is the position-sensing scheme.

Attached to the base of the vertical support dowel is a short arm with a small toy magnet attached. Directly below the magnet are eight magnetically activated reed switches. These switches are closed, one at a time, as the magnet moves over them. These switches are obtained, or can be removed from, inexpensive reed relays that are readily obtained from the local electronics supply store. If you choose to take apart reed relays, carefully remove the outer tape covering and coil until the reed switch is exposed. This reed is simply a small glass capsule with two magnetically operated contacts inside. By experimenting with the position of the magnets and the reeds, a point can be found where each of the main compass points (N, E, S, W), and intermediate points are triggered by the vane as it turns.

The circuit of the wind direction vane is given in Figure 60. It utilizes AC current and silicon diodes to allow 8 LEDs to be illuminated by the 8 reed switches as a function of wind position, with only

FIGURE 60

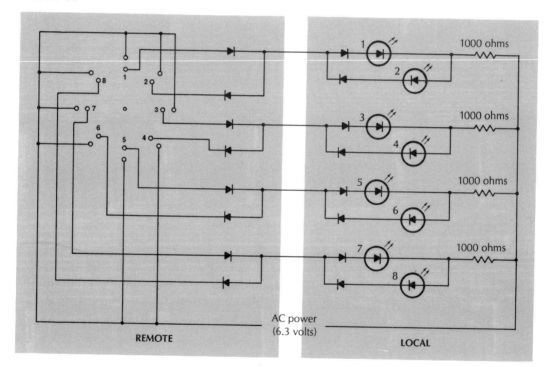

Circuit of Wind Direction Indicator

FIGURE 61

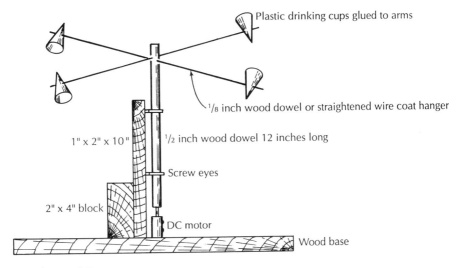

Plastic drinking cups glued to arms

¹/₈ inch wood dowel or straightened wire coat hanger

1" x 2" x 10"

¹/₂ inch wood dowel 12 inches long

Screw eyes

2" x 4" block

DC motor

Wood base

Wind Speed Detector

5 wires. When construction and alignment is finished, a small plastic food storage container, with a hole drilled in its bottom, is slipped over the vertical support as a weather resistant shield.

Wind speed is very easy to measure. Figure 61 shows a simple anemometer made of plastic drinking cups and wooden dowels. The vertical support shaft is of the same design as in the wind vane except that at the base is a small DC motor of the type that is found in many children's toys. This can be purchased at electronic supply stores and is inexpensive. The shaft of this motor is inserted into the end of the vertical dowel and centered so that the entire mechanism turns smoothly and freely. These motors make excellent generators of electrical current. When connected in a simple circuit such as Figure 62, they act as excellent speed indicators. The faster the cups turn, the higher the output voltage of the motor and the greater the deflection of the DC milliameter. The potentiometer or variable resistor is added to the circuit to enable it to be calibrated.

A quick way to calibrate the anemometer is to securely mount it to the hood of an automobile with strong but removable tape. Then

FIGURE 62

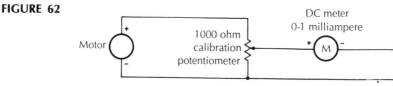

Circuit of Wind Speed Detector

have someone drive the automobile at steady speeds of 10, 20, 30, and 40 miles per hour while you adjust the potentiometer for full scale deflection at top speed and note the readings at the lower speeds. Of course, don't do this on a windy day. When you are finished, in-between points can be determined and either the meter scale recalibrated or a conversion chart made. When you have finished construction, a plastic food container can be used as a weather shield in the same manner as for the wind vane.

The measurement of rainfall is accomplished by a rain gauge that is nothing more than a large plastic pill container with a number of premeasured contacts set in it as per Figure 63. Each contact consists of a straight sewing pin with a short length of wire soldered to the top of it. While still hot, the pin is then pressed through the wall of the pill container and should "melt" its way in. These contacts are arranged at ¼-inch intervals with one pin at the very bottom for the common contact. Before use, the rain gauge is "primed" with a pinch of salt to improve conductivity. Figure 64 shows how transistors are used as

FIGURE 63

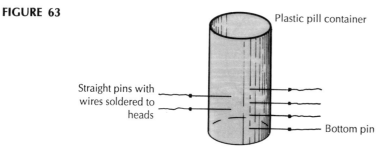

Rain Gauge Construction

FIGURE 64

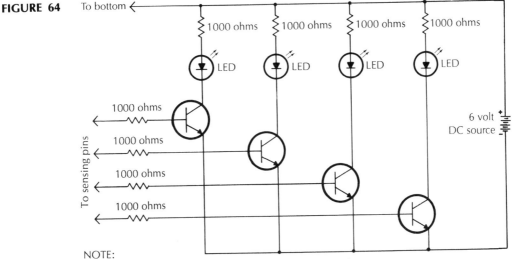

To bottom

1000 ohms 1000 ohms 1000 ohms 1000 ohms

LED LED LED LED

1000 ohms

6 volt
DC source

To sensing pins

1000 ohms

1000 ohms

1000 ohms

NOTE:
 All transistors are general purpose NPN, 2N2222 or similar.

Rain Gauge Circuit

sensors, and LEDs as indicators, for the water level. The rain gauge should be located where it can be easily emptied at the end of a rain period.

Sunlight intensity is measured with the circuit of Figure 47 in Chapter 7. A varnished cardboard tube is arranged so that the sensor points directly overhead, and a small piece of clear plastic food wrap is stretched and taped over the open end of the tube to prevent water and other materials from blocking the sensor. Then the unit is mounted in a location where there are no trees or other obstructions to block its view. Readings are taken on a regular basis to see how sunlight varies throughout the day. If the sensor is not moved, readings can even be taken from season to season to provide still more information. It is interesting to note that the sensor does not have to point to the sun. In fact, data will be more accurate if the unit *does not* point directly toward the sun. Figure 65 is a drawing of the sunlight sensor.

Once the individual sensors are built it is time to construct the

FIGURE 65

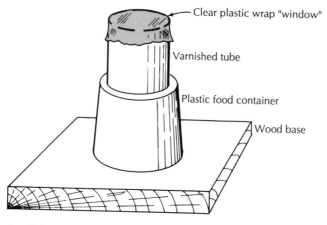

- Clear plastic wrap "window"
- Varnished tube
- Plastic food container
- Wood base

Sunlight Sensor

main display unit. Figure 66 shows what this can look like, although the experimenter can certainly vary the layout to meet his or her specific needs. The panel is made of ¼-inch plywood or masonite and the

FIGURE 66

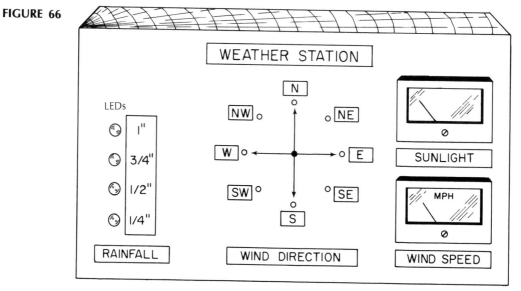

Typical Main Display Unit

base is made of 1-inch common pine. For a nice touch, the panel can even be made of a small piece of prefinished paneling. The exact method of finishing and labeling are left to the experimenter. The drawing is really just for reference.

Both the wind speed and sunlight intensity meters are imported 0 to 1 milliampere units that are readily available at the same electronics parts stores that supply the wire, LEDs, transformers, and other components.

As previously stated, build as much of the weather station as you wish. Each separate sensor is independent and can operate with or without the rest. When you are finished and have everything operating properly, it is interesting to begin keeping records of the various readings on a daily basis. By comparing your data with that given in the local newspapers, and by observing what actually happens with the weather, you may eventually be able to do a reasonably good job of forecasting conditions to come.

CHAPTER 9

ELECTRICITY AND PHOTOGRAPHY

It is interesting to note that avid electrical experimenters are usually interested in other creative hobbies as well. One such endeavor that seems to be somewhat more popular than the rest is amateur photography.

For the experimenter who shares both interests, there are several projects that will offer an extra measure of enjoyment since they satisfy the requirements of both hobbies. Commercial versions of the devices described below are available. However, the experimenter's versions work quite well and can be built for a fraction of the commercial equipment's cost.

One of the most common and widely used tools of the photographer is the light meter. This device is used constantly to determine the various camera settings for both normal and special situations. Commercial light meters are expensive, but they are not too different from our simple solar cell circuit of Figure 47. By some repackaging of the

FIGURE 67

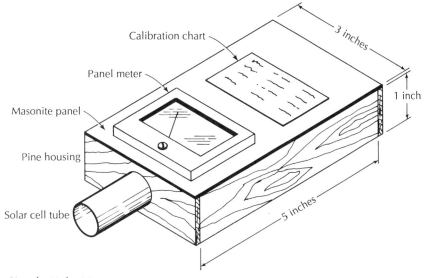

Simple Light Meter

circuit, as shown in Figure 67, a very acceptable light meter can be built. Leaving the solar cell tube open results in a wide acceptance angle. Fitting it with a short tube results in a more narrow angle. The key to making a meter that rivals commercial units is in calibration. If you can borrow a professional unit, you only have to compare readings on a point-by-point basis and copy the exposure/lens opening chart. Since there are no batteries to wear out or components to age, one careful calibration should result in a meter that will be accurate for years.

Just about everyone who takes photographs uses flash bulbs or electronic flash units. While the electronic flash units have a light that tells you when and if the flash is ready for use, cameras that use flash cubes or bulbs do not. If the batteries in such cameras are weak or defective, a good picture can be easily ruined.

Figure 68 is a very simple but useful flash tester for nonelectronic flash cameras. It is nothing more than a 115-volt to 6.3-volt transformer and a neon lamp. Its principle of operation is as simple as its

FIGURE 68

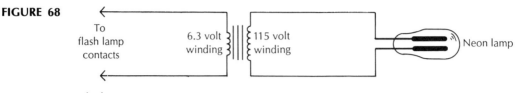

Flash Tester

circuit. The transformer is connected as a step-up unit with the low voltage winding connected to the camera's flash bulb contacts and the high voltage winding to the neon lamp. When the camera's shutter release button is pressed, a 3-volt pulse from the batteries in the camera is stepped up by the transformer to a 60-volt pulse, which is enough to cause the neon lamp to blink or flash. Since ample current is required to produce 3 volts across the transformer winding, only good batteries will pass this test. Weak or exhausted batteries will not produce enough current and the neon lamp will not blink.

Figure 69 shows the circuit of a remote flash unit that will be of use when making specialty photographs. The unit, or for that matter several units, can be placed anywhere within the range of the main flash unit connected to the camera. When the main flash unit fires, all of the various remote units will also fire, adding their light to the general illumination of the subject.

The remote flash unit uses a solar cell and transistor connected as a simple switch. When the light from the main flash strikes the cell, it triggers the transistor into conduction, firing the flash lamp within sev-

FIGURE 69

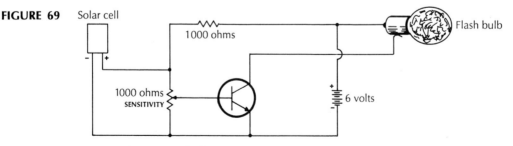

Circuit of Remote Flash Unit

MORE WIRES AND WATTS

eral *millionths of a second* from the start of the main flash. This is fast enough so that the camera integrates the light from all of the remote units with the light from the main unit into one total exposure.

Construction consists of mounting a socket that will fit the flash lamp desired, in the middle of a pie-plate reflector as shown in Figure 70. The transistor, potentiometer, and resistors are then soldered to wire brads and driven into the wood base as shown, with the battery holder. Four AA batteries (connected in series to achieve 6 volts) are used in this unit to assure enough current to fire the flash lamp.

When construction is finished, the remote flash can be tested by connecting a #47 lamp in place of the flash lamp and adjusting the variable resistor until a flashlight shining directly on the solar cell causes the #47 lamp to just light. You may have to "play" with this adjustment for the proper balance between the elimination of false

FIGURE 70

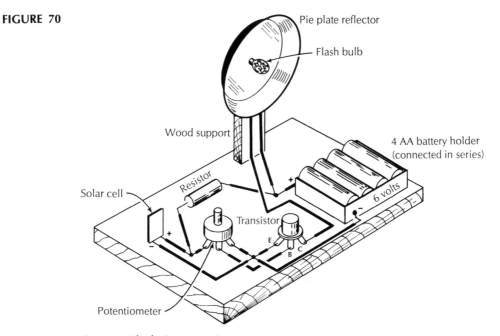

Remote Flash Construction

triggering due to stray light and reliable triggering from the main flash. To help make this adjustment less critical, add a cardboard tube to the solar cell with a short focal length "magnifying" lens glued to the tube end. In use, the only consideration is to assure a clear, unobstructed path between the solar cell and the main flash.

Electricity can help in taking some dramatic and unusual pictures. Have you ever wondered how a professional photographer takes a picture of the exact instant a ball hits a bucket of water or a pane of glass is struck with a stone? It's all done with triggering. Figure 71 shows the basic setup. As can be seen, a collimated light source such as a flashlight is arranged so that its beam shines directly on a solar cell. When this beam is broken by the object to be photographed, the solar cell triggers a transistor, which in turn triggers a second transistor and then the flash of the camera. The camera, in this case, is previously set so that its shutter is always open. The duration of the exposure is accomplished by the flash. Since most flashes last for less than $\frac{1}{100}$ of a second, the "stop action" is excellent. Of course, all of this must occur in darkness for it to work.

The circuit is straightforward and not too different from many of the others we have been building. The real trick here is in the care and thought given to the setup.

If you are careful and run through everything before opening the shutter, your chances of success are excellent.

FIGURE 71

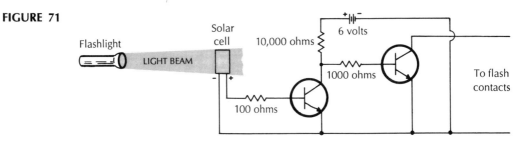

Exposure Trigger Circuit

CHAPTER **10**

FUN, GAMES, AND THINGS TO THINK ABOUT

If you have built the various projects described in the past nine chapters, you should be starting to understand what electricity is all about. By utilizing this knowledge, you can build some interesting games and puzzles as well as do some "original" research.

Figure 72 is a puzzle that can often stump the know-it-all in science class. As can be seen from the construction details, there are two boxes with two lamps and two switches and only one wire connecting all of them. Switch 1 controls lamp 1 while switch 2 controls lamp 2. There is absolutely no interaction between the two switches. When asked "How does it work?" some of the answers, even from experienced engineers, are often quite creative. Figure 73 shows how it really works, and the experimenter who may have forgotten some of the details should refer to Figure 37. Any opaque housing can be used for the boxes and #47 lamps will do nicely for the indicators. To make the puzzle appear more mysterious, the boxes might be interconnected with a single strand of #12 or #14 electrical house wire.

FIGURE 72

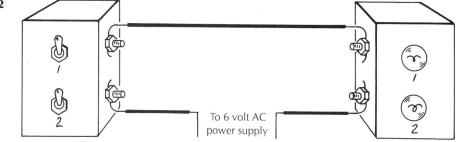

Two Lamp Puzzle

Figure 74 is a simple "tilt" sensor that can be the basis for all sorts of balancing devices. It consists of a relay, battery, buzzer, and sensor. The sensor, as shown in Figure 75, can take one of two forms. There is the hanging version, the sensitivity of which can be adjusted by the size of the sensing loop. The sensitivity of the steel ball version is a function of the depth of the hole the ball rests in. When either one of these is mounted in an opaque box with all of the circuitry, the results can be a lot of fun. The steel ball, by the way, can usually be obtained from dealers or repair shops that specialize in older style electromechanical pinball machines.

An interesting game that will be of use in fund-raising carnivals is the "coin pitching" unit of Figure 76. This is a lot more difficult to beat than appears at first and really "pulls" people in. It is made by gluing

FIGURE 73

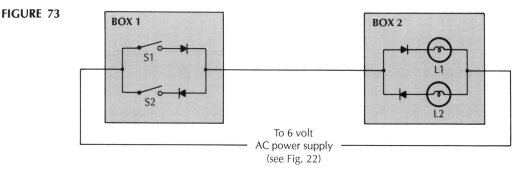

Circuit of Two Lamp Puzzle

FIGURE 74

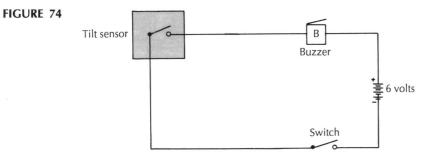

Tilt sensor   B   Buzzer   6 volts   Switch

Circuit of Tilt Sensor

aluminum foil onto a suitably sized wooden base and then carefully cutting out a number of concentric circles in the foil with a sharp hobby knife. Wiring these in the simple circuit shown, with a number of lamps and doorbell-type buzzers, results in a very professional attraction. Be certain that the gap cut between the foil circles is about ⅛-inch wide and that the width of the foil between the gaps is at least 2 to 3 inches. After building the unit, dress it up with a fancy design and bright colors painted in the various foil gaps. Be certain not to get paint onto the aluminum foil contacts, however.

FIGURE 75

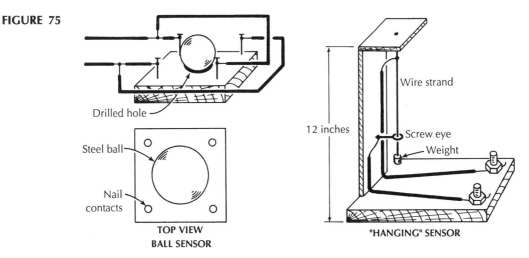

Drilled hole

Steel ball

Nail contacts

**TOP VIEW
BALL SENSOR**

Wire strand

12 inches

Screw eye

Weight

"HANGING" SENSOR

Two Types of Tilt Sensors

FUN, GAMES, AND THINGS TO THINK ABOUT   **73**

FIGURE 76

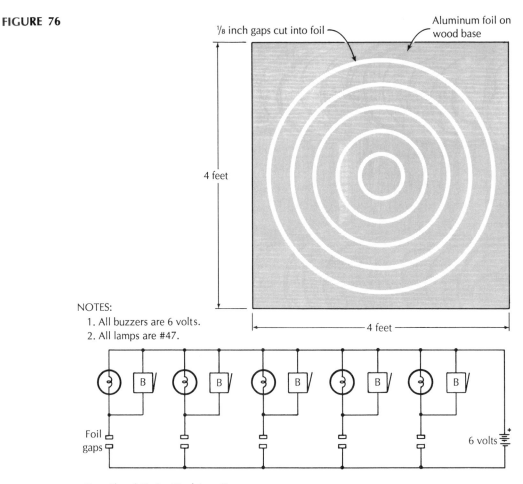

NOTES:
1. All buzzers are 6 volts.
2. All lamps are #47.

Details of Coin Pitching Game

In the early 1900s, when the wonders of electricity were just be-ginning to be appreciated, a number of experiments were conducted to see if plant growth could be influenced by the application of elec-trical currents. While the results stated then seemed impressive, the idea never seemed to catch on and the technique is not in use today. Does it really work? Only recently have scientists begun using electric currents to help heal broken bones and torn ligaments. One would therefore think that these same currents might aid in the growth of plants.

Figure 77 is a wooden planting box that the experimenter can easily build to test the results of electric currents on plants. It is quite conventional except for the sides and bottom. These are covered with thin aluminum plates, brought out to terminals as shown. The aluminum is roofing flashing, readily obtainable at hardware stores, and is very easy to cut with a strong pair of scissors. When the box is built, it should be filled with clean potting soil and some quickly growing seeds such as lima beans or peas. The experimenter, under his own guidelines, should then apply a continuous electrical current between several plates, as desired, and see what happens. Experiments should be performed with both AC and DC, keeping accurate records of results, and some new principle may actually be discovered. The plants

FIGURE 77

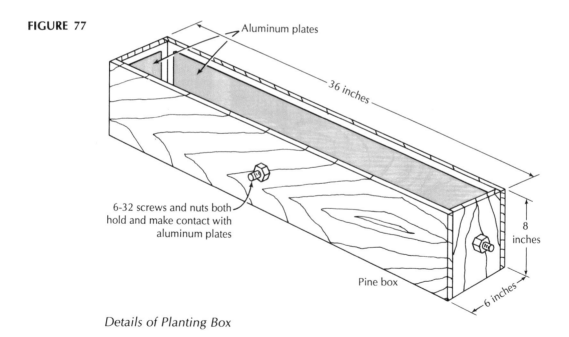

Aluminum plates

36 inches

6-32 screws and nuts both hold and make contact with aluminum plates

8 inches

Pine box

6 inches

Details of Planting Box

should be watered regularly and subjected to the same care that is given to regular house plants. For the source of current, only the 6-volt AC or DC power sources described in the book should be used. Furthermore, a lamp of the proper voltage should be connected in series with the power source used to prevent damage to the source in the event of an accidental short circuit. (A lamp used in this manner is called a limit resistor.) If results are obtained that seem interesting, the experiments should be repeated. If desired, another planting box, built and planted with the same type of plants as the first box may be constructed (but without the electrical current) as a way of evaluating the actual effect of the current. The box with the current is the experiment, while the box without the current is called the control.

In an even more "way out" area, the experimenter can investigate the ESP (extrasensory perception) sensitivity of various people as well as try to determine whether telekinesis, or "mind over matter," really exists.

The ESP tester consists of a series of ten switches, arranged in two

FIGURE 78

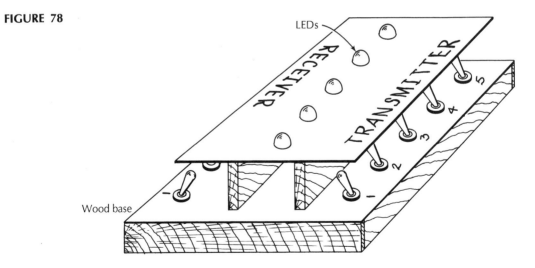

Details of ESP Tester

FIGURE 79

NOTE:
All LED's are general purpose types.

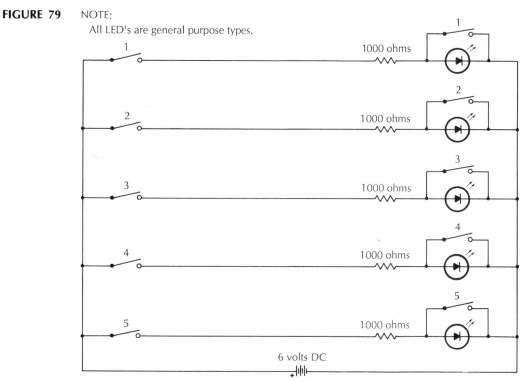

Circuit of ESP Tester

groups of five as shown in Figure 78. The barrier blocks the "transmitter's" switches from being seen by the "receiver." In operation, the person who is the "transmitter" closes a switch and projects his or her thoughts to the "receiver" person. When the "receiver" thinks he or she knows which switch was closed, he or she activates the corresponding switch. A correct guess lights the LED associated with the switch. By keeping accurate records of 100 or more tries by various persons, the experimenter might be able to find someone with great ESP "sensitivity," someone who does much better than the average person. The circuit of the ESP tester is given in Figure 79. Note that the "transmitter's" switches are normally open and select the proper LED.

The "receiver's" switches are normally closed and short circuit the LEDs until opened. The resistors limit the battery current to the LEDs and shorts. The switches are common SPST toggle switches and the LEDs are inexpensive, general purpose indicators. A 6-volt lantern battery is used as a long lasting source of power.

Testing "mind over matter" is a little more difficult. Any motion actually caused by a person as a result of thought is bound to be very small, if it exists at all, so a sensitive detector of motion is necessary. Figure 80 is such a unit. In a manner similar to the tilt sensor described earlier in this chapter, a brass weight is suspended on a fine wire in the

FIGURE 80

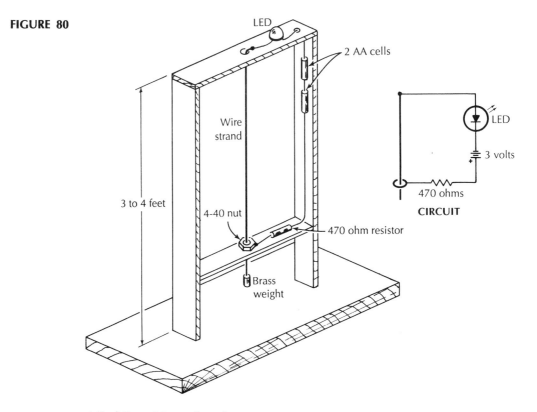

Mind-Over-Matter Experiment

center of a small nut. The system is then carefully adjusted so that the slightest movement causes the wire to contact the nut and the circuit to be completed. The wire is a single strand of common electrical "zip cord" and should be at least 3 to 4 feet long. The support should be as stable as possible and placed on the ground for even more stability. Finally, a plastic food container should be arranged around the contacts to prevent air currents from triggering the circuit. At this point, various people should be encouraged to try to complete the circuit with their thoughts.

Variations and improvements on many of the devices described in this book will no doubt occur to the reader. The author heartily encourages the implementation of these ideas and hopes that the various chapters serve merely as starting points for a whole series of enjoyable endeavors.

WHATEVER YOU DO, ALWAYS KEEP SAFETY IN MIND. AS WONDERFUL AS ELECTRICITY CAN BE, IT CAN ALSO BE DANGEROUS. NEVER WORK DIRECTLY WITH THE AC POWER LINE AND ALWAYS RECHECK ALL CONNECTIONS AT LEAST TWICE BEFORE APPLYING POWER TO ANY CIRCUIT. The rest is up to you.

index